HELP!
my halo's slipping

Larry Dinkins

AN OMF BOOK

HELP! MY HALO'S SLIPPING

© OMF INTERNATIONAL
(*formerly China Inland Mission*)

Published by Overseas Missionary Fellowship (USA) Inc.
10 W. Dry Creek Circle, Littleton, CO 80120

First published 1990
This printing 2006

ISBN 9971-972-96-4

OMF Books are distributed by
OMF, 10 West Dry Creek Circle, Littleton, CO 80120, USA
OMF, Station Approach, Borough Green, Sevenoaks, Kent TN15 8BG, United Kingdom
OMF, PO Box 849, Epping, NSW 2121, Australia
OMF, 5155 Spectrum Way, Bldg 21, Mississauga, ON L4W 5A1 Canada
OMF, PO Box 10159, Auckland, New Zealand
and other OMF offices

Cover photos by Kevin Morris and Adam Weathered
Cover design by Tony Waghorn, OMF UK

CONTENTS

INTRODUCTION

*"Grow in the grace and knowledge of our
Lord and Savior Jesus Christ"
(2 Peter 3:18).*

Michael, who had been in Thailand only two months, poured out his confusion and frustration in a jumble of questions. "How long did it take to get the language? Why do the Thai act the way they do? Did you ever feel homesick? How long until Thailand begins to feel like home?

Such questions were all too familiar. As a new worker I too had puzzled over the same issues.

I explained to Michael that what he was experiencing was neither unusual nor uncommon. Such "growing pains" often accompany cultural adjustment and are the shared experience of most new workers. Michael was undergoing what I call a "ripening" process. In Thailand young men who have not yet entered the Buddhist monkhood are called *khon dip* meaning "raw, green, un-initiated". Those who have completed the rites are called *khon suk*, "ripened ones". Similar words are used when describing one of the few fruits that ripens off the vine — the banana.

Like the banana, the missionary is germinated and grows in the protected greenhouse of his home environment. Finally ties with the mother plant are cut and the "green" recruit is transplanted to a foreign shore. There he slowly ripens, until at the end of a four-year term he is considered ripe, thus earning the ominous title: "senior missionary".

For a banana the ripening process is painless and quick. For a new missionary, passing from green to yellow can be fraught with problems and takes years not days. First terms are notorious periods of internal turmoil, external threats, and personal adjustments. The first term of the founder of my mission, James Hudson Taylor, is a prime example. During his first six years in China Taylor had recurring illness, financial problems, and robbery. Later his mission society failed him and he was forced to resign. Worst of all, his associates criticized him bitterly for adopting Chinese dress.

Jonah, reluctant missionary to the Ninevites, is another example. After only one day of ministry an entire city of possibly 600,000 people was converted. In contrast, Jonah's "conversion" was like pulling teeth — time-consuming and excruciatingly painful. Someone rightly observed, "God can convert a national in an instant, but it may take years to convert a missionary."

This ripening process is not limited to missionaries but can be seen in secular professions — politics, for example. John F. Kennedy started his first and only term in 1960 as a young visionary with grand schemes for what America could become. His optimism was no doubt based on the success he experienced as a decorated naval officer and as a Congressman. Yet over the next three years, Kennedy's tenure was littered with messy crises — in Cuba, Laos, Vietnam, Congo, Latin America, and Berlin. After weathering these storms a more sober Kennedy said, "There is no experience you can get that can possibly prepare you adequately for the presidency."

It took all of those events, both bitter and sweet, to mature J F Kennedy as president and as a man.

The same is true of the missionary. No experience can prepare you adequately for the mission field. No one arrives on the field as a "ripened" banana. God has His own unique methods to bring about maturity during those early years; at times He may use "messy crises" and at others simply "irritations". However, the ultimate goal is always the same, "... to a mature man, to the measure of the stature which belongs to the fulness of Christ" (Eph. 4:13).

Every first termer is in a "sink or swim" situation. It reminds me of the approved method of teaching swimming in Thailand. Many Thai live along the waterways or even on rafts and rice barges. Often you will see very small children enjoying a dip on a hot afternoon. There are no YMCAs around to teach swimming. The student (maybe only three or four years old) is put in water over his head and either swims or sinks. A parent is close by in the latter case!

A new worker's introduction to missionary life is just as traumatic. Suddenly he is thrown headlong into a new culture, climate, lifestyle and language. What was merely theory at home becomes harsh reality in the daily grind of life on the field. What's more, Mommy and Daddy are nowhere to be found as the waters of frustration, sickness, and separation begin to rise. The mission agency may give a few pointers, but basically you have one term to either swim or sink.

What follows is an account of the "swimming lesson", the "ripening process", God gave the Dinkins family during our first term as church planters in central Thailand. Our family had a lot to learn, for rarely has a family arrived in Thailand as *dip* as ours. Once we lost an entire night's sleep simply from ignorance of how to use a mosquito net! Without the Lord we would have drowned amid the swirling currents of cultural change, language learning and satanic opposition. With Him we have learned to swim. He never let us drop headlong over the falls, but placed boulders in strategic places to give us rest amid the waves. We haven't yet crossed the sea of cultural change but praise God we are still swimming ... and learning.

If you picked up this book thinking it was a Victorian missionary biography portraying the glamorous and adventuresome lives of haloed saints sacrificing life and limb on a heathen shore ... then think again. You will find that missionaries are cut from the same bolt of cloth as yourself. They have the same fears, interpersonal problems, inferiority feelings and worries as the rest of mankind. When you cut them they bleed. As you get to know us you will discover that missionaries are indeed ordinary people.

ONE

COURTSHIP

Two are better than one, because they have a good return for their
work ... A cord of three strands is not quickly broken.
(Eccles 4: 9.12)

A cultural shift occurred on college campuses throughout America in the early 1970's. The idealistic activism of
the turbulent sixties was waning. Students began to
settle into a philosophy of apathy. Education was merely
a means to the ultimate goal — making money. The
other major pursuit was the pleasure cult of wine (or
drugs), women and song. At Oklahoma University the
Greek system of fraternities and sororities seemed to
offer the best of both worlds.

I was one of those students, and so was Paula, although we had not yet met. At that time the thought of
becoming a committed Christian, much less a missionary, was humorous to say the least. For me the plan was
a comfortable career in banking; for Paula, a career in
teaching and the prospect of marriage. Something
radical would have to happen to alter the course of our
lives at this point.

As pledge trainer of the Delta Gamma Sorority, Paula
was in charge of 25 freshman girls. When two staff workers from Campus Crusade for Christ requested a meeting, Paula agreed, thinking it would be good to have at

least one "religious" meeting that year. Yet it was Paula who responded to the invitation to trust Christ. At that point she was engaged to a non-Christian and only a few months away from marriage. Her decision to follow Christ landed like a bombshell on their relationship. Paula's fiancé gave her an ultimatum, saying, "Christians only live to die". All marriage plans were canceled, even though the wedding dress had been tried on and date set.

My experience was similiar but not so dramatic. A student in a rival fraternity simply shared a gospel tract, saw some potential, and asked me to join his discipleship group. What followed for both of us was a year of incubation in which the gospel seed, germinated under the campus ministry and watered by the local church, began to take root and grow in our lives.

It was at this juncture that Paula's life and mine intersected for the first time. While on the rebound from her broken engagement, Paula attended a birthday party for a Christian coed in her sorority. As the only male attending, I was asked to bless the food. As I finished my prayer, Paula began a silent one of her own, "Lord, someday I would like to have a friend like Larry, but for now I am content just knowing you."

During the next year we dated sporadically, but remained merely "brother and sister" in Christ. Then one day Paula invited me to her apartment for a Bible study over omelets. This combination proved fatal — experiencing Paula's culinary skills and seeing her respond to spiritual input showed me that this relationship was destined to go deeper.

Graduation from college in 1975, however, brought a momentary interruption to our relationship. Both of us needed to make difficult career decisions. Paula wondered whether she should pursue teaching as a profession or volunteer for Christian ministry. Then God led her to apply for Campus Crusade staff, and she was sent to their headquarters two thousand miles away in California. For the moment we would have to be content with being pen pals.

As I contemplated whether to go on staff with Campus Crusade or start in business, a friend shocked me with the question, "Larry, what do you want to be in thirty years?" As a typical college student I was used to setting short term goals, until the next test or semester break. Planning long range was new to me. My friend suggested I attend Bible school. That way I could lay a biblical foundation for my life, no matter what field I chose to pursue. At his direction I applied to Dallas Theological Seminary and was accepted.

Like most seminary students I began to dream of being a spellbinding preacher or noted scholar. This was only natural, since all my role models and heroes were either pastors or professors. Missions wasn't an option. In fact, during my first missions course the students were asked to list "reasons why you wouldn't want to be a missionary" — I came up with nine! It took a simple challenge from a missions speaker to remove these excuses and put me on a road that would eventually lead to Thailand.

During missions week, a speaker from the Overseas Missionary Fellowship asked the students how many were interceding daily for a missionary by name. A few hands went up — but not mine. Don't get me wrong; I did pray for missions. Yet asking God "to bless all the missionaries in Africa" was obviously not what the speaker had in mind by "intercession". At the end of his lecture, the speaker handed out prayer commitment cards. Little did I realize the impact that little blue card would have.

Within days I received information concerning Dr Henry Breidenthal, a graduate of my seminary as well as a medical doctor and linguist. After six years of tribal and medical ministry, Dr Henry moved to Bangkok and in 1971 started the Bangkok Bible College. I set about lifting Dr Henry up to God daily, even though my knowledge was limited to a card with his picture on it.

In God's timing I began to attend an OMF monthly prayer meeting as a way to further my growing interest in Asia. At one memorable meeting I poured out my heart to God for Dr Breidenthal, mentioning the problems I imagined that he and his wife and children were encountering in that Buddhist stronghold. It was then that a veteran missionary pulled me aside and gently whispered in my ear, "Larry, Dr Henry is single."

The host of the meeting was Louis Almond. Before retiring, the Almonds served in China and Thailand for a total of 71 years. Stella introduced me to spicy Thai curry, and Louis to the tremendous needs of Thailand. I'll never forget the night he shared that only .1% of the 50 million Thai were Protestant Christians, and that Buddhist temples alone numbered close to 30,000 while Protestant membership was a meager 60,000. These prayer warriors showed a genuine concern for people far removed in time and space and yet close to the Savior's heart.

I am convinced that where your prayer interest lies, there your heart lies also. I found it impossible to pray daily that God would meet the spiritual needs in Thailand, without myself becoming involved. Yes, prayer is dangerous. The more I prayed for Thailand the more uneasy I felt about filling a pulpit in the States. Even a teaching position lost its luster. Each time I knelt to pray for Thailand on the multicolored patchwork rug in the Almonds' converted garage, a struggle ensued:

Larry:	"Oh God, send someone to reach the Thai people."
God:	"Well, Larry, what are you doing now?"
Larry:	"I'm preparing to be a minister, Lord."
God:	"That's right, why don't you go to Thailand?"
Larry:	"But you know how I had my heart set on a pastorate or teaching position."
God:	"Don't worry, you can preach and lecture over there. Just leave the rest to me."

Slowly the misconceptions and arguments against missions that I had built up in my mind began to fade. Missionary biographies which before seemed dry and boring sprang to life. Books like *Hudson Taylor's Spiritual Secret, Shadow of the Almighty* by Elizabeth Elliot, and *Have We No Rights* helped me see the true nature of mission work. A missionary wasn't some safari-suited warrior complete with pith helmet and machete, cutting his way through the jungle in search of an unreached tribe. He need not be a super saint or even a holy hero. What God wanted from me was not my *abilities* — they tend to get in the way. What God wanted was my *availability*, my willingness to follow Christ wherever He might lead — even overseas.

"A boat trip does not make you a missionary." I knew that if I planned to minister overseas I would need to be a missionary on the homeside first. My church already had an outreach to the neglected and unreached in the community. During Sunday School a team from church would hold services in the local jail or black community. I tried my hand at open air preaching, and spent a weekend with a fellow student in downtown Dallas, living like street people on only $4. I never will forget that first sleepless night in the bus terminal, standing in chow lines, or the night we spent in the Dallas Rescue Mission (we never did convince the directors that we were actually seminary students).   In retrospect, such experiences among disadvantaged Americans helped prepare me for future ministry among underprivileged poor in Thai society — the leprosy sufferers who made up the majority in the church in central Thailand.

Meanwhile, Paula, as a receptionist with Campus Crusade, was being exposed to missionaries from around the world.   Her Sunday school teacher was Arthur Mathews, who had been one of the last two members of the China Inland Mission to leave the interior of China after months of house arrest under the communists. Arthur gave Paula a copy of *Green Leaf in Drought* which details their year-long trial of fire in China.   The Lord used the Mathews to increase Paula's awareness of the spiritual drought in East Asia as well as the principles of the OMF.

God, who had untangled the frayed and confused strands of our two lives, began to gently bring those strands together in marriage.   At the same time He was adding a third strand to strengthen the relationship — a common burden for missions.   Our long-distance love affair would eventually last three years, running up large phone bills and consuming reams of correspondence. Paula's acceptance of my proposal in October of 1977 was followed by our wedding the next spring.   Leaving the security of family and ministry in California for an uncertain future in Texas was heart-wrenching for Paula. This experience would be repeated time and again in the coming years.

Our next leap of faith concerned the choice of a missions board.   After years of "dating" OMF, observing its missionaries and studying its distinctives, we decided to take the plunge and apply.   A preliminary form was followed up by a battery of questionnaires and tests. Courting OMF through the mail was nearly as frustrating as courting Paula had been. Our knowledge of OMF was incomplete and certain questions had to be answered before we could commit ourselves. Only a first-hand exposure would suffice. This opportunity came at the OMF candidate school held at Robesonia, Pennsylvania in June 1979.

TWO

ENGAGEMENT

*We need young people, healthy, intelligent, committed; divergent
thinkers who will say "Why not ...?" rather than "How can ...?"
People whose passionate purpose, like ours, is the urgent
evangelization of East Asia's millions.
(One Passionate Purpose — OMF Booklet)*

I had been told that the proper procedure for getting
engaged was as follows: movie, candlelight dinner, followed by the presentation of a ring. I had every intention of following this procedure; but circumstances forced
me to "pop the question" via a long distance phone call.
Formal engagement with a candlelight dinner and ring
presentation came two months later. Those two months
gave me plenty of time to reflect on the step I had taken.
Like most fiancés, I had the emotion of excitement
mixed with a fair bit of trepidation.

Attending the OMF candidate school evoked similar
feelings. Both Paula and I were thrilled with the prospect of ministry in Asia, yet sobered by the enormity of
the step. Like other candidates before us, we had both
real and imagined fears, questions, and misgivings. After
two years of "dating" OMF we would finally see the
organization at close range and in depth.

Our group of candidates consisted of six couples and
a single man. Most were in their late twenties and had

experience in both secular business and ministry. Although coming from different parts of the country, all were attracted, as I was, by the ethos of OMF: a passion for the unreached, simple lifestyle, financial policies and faith in God to supply. The ethos of OMF is best symbolized in its insignia — two cupped hands reaching heavenward, with arrows pointing downward indicating answered prayer. This emblem can be found on everything from Land Rovers to pendants. It graphically shows OMF's dependence on Jehovah Jireh — its founder Hudson Taylor's favorite name for God, "the Lord will provide".

At times I wondered if my head would explode from the amount of information we were exposed to in just three weeks. We had lectures on OMF distinctives and the famous "P and P" — Principles and Practice. We used the library to fulfill reading assignments and do field research on our country of interest. Bible studies and times of prayer were another highlight. On Sundays we made trips to local churches for ministry and spent one morning at Lammermuir House in Lancaster Pennsylvania. This home for retired missionaries was named after the ship which took the first party of CIM to China in 1866. Like the rest of the candidates, I was impressed with their knowledge of the various fields and their continued burden to pray.

The lectures and assignments were easy compared to the interviews. The final interview was before the national council, a board of twelve professionals, including doctors, missionaries, educators, businessmen and pastors. Their goal is to confirm that God is really calling this candidate to Asia through OMF. I expected a "hot seat" treatment similiar to the ordination exam I passed just weeks before. To my surprise no one grilled me under a harsh light in a darkened room. It was more like a friendly chit-chat. I could tell by their questions that people had a genuine desire to send laborers to the harvest fields. I left that room with a sigh of relief that the last hurdle was past.

Two other couples, however, encountered hurdles which they were not able to surmount and decided not to affiliate with OMF. Such a decision is never easy, especially when you have come so far in the screening process. The reasons vary. Sometimes it is a health matter, doctrinal issue or psychological concern. Some parents cannot accept the possible need of boarding school for their children. Having struggled through some of these issues ourselves helped us sympathize with those who were redirected. Our direction, however, was clear. Candidate school gave us the calm assurance that God was indeed calling us to Asia with OMF.

James Hudson Taylor, in the year he founded the China Inland Mission, 1865, wrote this phrase in the margin of his Bible, "Prayed for 24 willing, skillful workers." God was still calling out workers in answer to prayer 114 years later. The nine remaining candidates in our group gave testimony to that fact. I'm glad Dr Taylor mentioned "willing" first before "skillful". Availability is the main ingredient in missionary service. I'm convinced God will provide the "skills" and gifts as long as we stay available to doing His will.

Two years of dating OMF and a three-week engagement at candidate school finally climaxed in a wedding — a dedication ceremony at a nearby church. At this ceremony nine of us were "wedded" to the mission and formally accepted as Appointees. Instead of a wedding march we sang this long-time favorite of CIM-OMF:

> *How good is the God we adore!*
> *Our faithful, unchangeable friend;*

His love is as great as His power,
And knows neither measure nor end.

Tis Jesus the first and the last;
Whose Spirit shall guide us safe home;
We'll praise Him for all that is past,
And trust Him for all that's to come.

The final stage before leaving for the field is like being "newly wed". The flurry of excitement which surrounded the engagement and climaxed with the wedding is still fresh, yet it is tempered by the reality of "married life" — building a prayer and financial support base and gaining ministry experience before leaving for the field. This stage is commonly called deputation.

In the course of one year we visited a variety of churches spread over six states. Our travels took us all the way from laid-back country churches in Oklahoma to high-strung megachurches in California. At each stop we were impressed with the hospitality and love of mission minded believers.

While living in a trailer park in Dallas we got a taste of mission work — every trailer but ours was occupied by a Jehovah's Witness family! Trying to share Christ in that environment was difficult, but nothing compared to what we would be facing in Buddhist Thailand.

When we moved to Oklahoma an opportunity to gain experience in church planting arose. A newly formed church meeting in a upholstery shop needed help so I agreed to act as assistant pastor. The church had only fifteen adults, but its bus ministry served one hundred children. Planting this church, purchasing land, and helping erect a building was similar to what I would later do on the field. The opportunity to start from scratch and work our way up proved invaluable.

Another goal was to start an OMF prayer meeting in our home. There are presently over 250 similiar meetings throughout the United States. One of our most faithful prayer warriors was "Aunt Stubby" — 90 year old Caroline Studdiford. Although confined to a nursing home and crippled, Aunt Stubby carried on correspondence with two hundred missionaries scattered around the world. By the time we left for Asia another 200 prayer supporters had committed themselves to our ministry. The knowledge that this band of men and women was lifting up our specific needs to God was a constant source of strength and encouragement throughout our first term.

J O Fraser, apostle to the Lisu tribe in China, saw the necessity of prayer support from the homeside when he wrote to his mother, "I know that you will never fail me in the matter of intercession, but would you think and pray about getting a group of like-minded friends, whether few or many, whether in one place or scattered, to join in the same petitions? If you could form a small prayer circle I would write regularly to the members."[1]

Our desire to secure prayer supporters increased when we learned that twenty OMFers had died through martyrdom or accident in Thailand over the last thirty years. Only two years before, five members of the medical staff in central Thailand were killed in a traffic accident.

During our year of deputation OMF made it clear that Paula would have to make up a deficiency in Bible courses. The mission wanted to make sure that all new workers knew how to feed themselves from the Word of God. There were no "fast food" Bible outlets on the plains of central Thailand. Our own spiritual vitality and

---

[1] J O Fraser's story is told in *Mountain Rain* (OMF Books)

that of our congregation depended on our ability to nourish ourselves from the Word of God.

C T Studd advised a new recruit, "Read and prepare practically. Above all, read your Bible and get a practical knowledge of it. It is not biblical lollipops that are of use out here, but good healthy chunks to pelt the devil with and feed the hungry souls around one."

OMF leaders had made it clear at the candidate course that Paula was to be accepted on her own merits. She couldn't go to Thailand on the basis of my call. Some couples have had to return home because the wife thought she could enter the mission field on the shirt-tails of a gifted husband. Not so. Hudson Taylor laid that principle down a hundred years ago, "It is most important that married missionaries should be double missionaries not half or a quarter or eighth-part mission-aries ... Unless you intend your wife to be a true mission-ary, not merely a wife, homemaker, and friend, *do not* join us."

A real highlight of our deputation time was meeting Thai people here in the States. Who would guess that Nat Siriwat, the son of a former Thai ambassador to France, would be studying in my hometown — Shawnee, Oklahoma. When we found Nat a Bible he responded, "You know, I've never seen a Bible in Thai before." Nat was studying political science and was eager to tell us about the government, culture and history of Thailand.

Shawnee also boasted a pair of Thai medical doctors. Even though they had worked in a Christian hospital they had never heard the gospel clearly. They thought it strange that we should go to such an underdeveloped country, which they had left a decade before. Their reaction was similiar to the man in Thailand who asked, "Why do you have to stoop to this kind of work? Is it because you couldn't find anything to do in your own country?" Sharing Christ with Thai in "Christian" America gave us a feel for how difficult it would be to share Christ in Buddhist Thailand.

The final week before departure for our orientation course in Singapore was physically and emotionally exhausting. One day Paula witnessed a crime while jogging in the neighborhood, and had to go through police questioning. When that was cleared up she had to organize a garage sale and stow our entire household. She found it particularly difficult packing unused wedding gifts. Packing for the field made us better appreciate the simple lifestyle principle stressed by the mission.

Finally, the night before our flight to Asia we had a chance to reflect. Lying in bed that quiet spring night, Paula turned to me and blurted out, "Larry, I'm scared." Both of us were feeling the enormity of the step we were about to take. 83-year-old Jemima Schreiber had given us a very appropriate verse to claim as we left for the field. It was the same verse she had claimed before leaving for China in the early 1920's: Deuteronomy 31:8, "And the Lord is the one who goes ahead of you; He will be with you. He will not fail or forsake you. Do not fear, or be dismayed."

My family was strangely quiet as we rode to the airport for the first leg of our trip to Singapore. Words were few as we walked down the sloping ramp, past the metal detector and into the lounge area. Finally, my 76-year-old grandfather broke the silence. Turning to my father he said, "This is worse than when you went to war, Merle." Granddad was right: our future was uncertain and unpredictable. But it was controlled by a certain and predictable God who promised never to fail or forsake us.

I have a snapshot of our family in the departure lounge that day. On the outside we appear to be smiling, but believe me, on the inside we felt like a wrung-out dishrag. As we entered the plane I saw something I had never seen in my previous 26 years — dad was crying.

THREE

HONEYMOON BEGINS

Jack:	*"What's this?"*
Englishman:	*"Why, it's leg of lamb, of course."*
Jack:	*"It's kind of bland isn't it?"*
Englishman:	*"Why don't you try some mint sauce on it?"*
Jack:	*"Naw, what this needs is some ketchup."*
Englishman:	*"Excuse me, but we English never put ketchup on lamb!"*
Jack:	*"Well, here's one American who does!"*

Before we left for Asia, Jack Largent related this incident from his own time in orientation course, as a means of preparing this family of Americans for Singapore. I can't say I was ever served lamb, but like Jack I had a lot of adjustments to make during our orientation course.

At the airport in Singapore we were relieved to notice the familiar initials OMF on the shirt of a tall missionary standing in line to greet us. Groggy from a fifteen hour flight, we gratefully accepted his hospitality. We were lucky; other new missionaries would be in the air more than twice as long.

Our host drove us through the bustling city of Singapore until we came to a palm-lined drive leading to a cream-colored two story bungalow topped by red tiles and framed by climbing bouganvillea. 2 Cluny Road is the international nerve center of OMF, set on two acres of choice land across from the Botanical Gardens.

In 1952, after the mission had to leave China, the leaders established its headquarters in Singapore to maintain Hudson Taylor's principle of headquarters being on the field. This insures that policy decisions are made in Asia rather than in a western culture, and allows Asian leaders to have input also.

Recently much of the original facilities we enjoyed were cleared away to make room for a new million dollar complex which the mission hopes will become the Antioch of Asia, a key sending center to turn out an ever increasing number of young recruits for the harvest fields of Asia.

Our host led us to two breezy rooms with ceiling fans. The closets had built-in light bulbs which were on all the time. I thought it was strange until my favorite pair of sandals turned green — the light bulbs are there to counteract mold. Tiny lizards called geckos greeted us from their upside-down world on the ceiling. We were prepared for the worst but were pleasantly surprised at the surroundings. Paula wrote home, "There are orchids and mosquito nets in each room. So far so good!"

For the next two and a half months 2 Cluny Road would be our home as we completed what is called Orientation Course — OMF's boot camp for new recruits. The goal is simple: orient the new worker to the orient. First, to become acquainted with OMF and its ethos; secondly, to adjust to cross cultural community living; and thirdly, attain basic skills in phonetics and culture. We heard lectures on a plethora of subjects, from stress to spirits, from geography to religion.

By far the talk that stirred the most interest was Dr

Hogben's "Deadly Disease" lecture. It reminded me of a horror movie I had seen as a youth. The diminutive Dr Monica crammed a whole semester of tropical diseases into a single lecture. For a solid hour she spoke of impetigo, typhoid, cholera, along with mites, ticks, and mosquitos, without even a squirm. At one point she drew a foot-long roundworm on the blackboard, claiming that 90% of the world's population contracts worms at one time or another.

Other lectures touched on the political situation in Asia. I asked an expert on military history about the situation in Thailand. He replied, "Thailand is like a melting pot about to boil," which wasn't too comforting. His words were prophetic because within months of our arrival there was a major military coup. A Buddhist monk advised us to forget about trying to evangelize Buddhists. "Pour yourself into social work, that is where you will do the most good."

I don't remember much from the various lectures, but one phrase used by a veteran tribal worker from north Thailand stood out, "Be a missionary who oils the works, not grit." He was right; I have observed that those with a positive attitude usually survive, but those with a negative, gritty personality frequently flounder.

A primary stress of the Orientation Course was language acquisition. This required 22 sessions on phonetics. Imagine thirteen adults wearing headphones trying to pronounce thousands of nonsense syllables like "jpjxat-apadata".

As language learners, we found Singapore a linguistic paradise. We attended a Presbyterian church which had services in five languages. Street signs were often written in all four of the Republic's official languages.

The linguistic courses were difficult, to be sure, but as a monolingual "Okie" (Oklahoman) I found communication within the mission almost as difficult.

Take meals for instance. Once I asked for a cookie I spied on the table. After groping for a moment came the reply, "Oh, you mean biscuits. Sure, here you are." Later I saw some biscuits (American) on the table and, determined not to repeat my previous mistake, asked politely, "Please pass the cookies."

Helen from New Zealand replied, "Pass the what?"

"The cookies," I said.

Finally, Helen said, "No, no, these aren't cookies — they're *scones!*"

At the end of the course I had increased my vocabulary fivefold and could tell you the difference between a loo and a lift, a boot and a bonnet and even chips and crisps. My English friends warned me about using the word "bugger" but they would turn around and call someone a "silly ass" without flinching!

In a sense we all had to adjust to two cultures — an international mission and the local culture. In Singapore you don't blow your nose in a restaurant, point your fingers or offer a gift with your left hand. In OMF you avoided putting ketchup on lamb or calling trousers "pants" (which is underwear to the British). Even reading the calendar demanded an adjustment. Everyone knows that 7-4-84 means July fourth 1984, right? Wrong. The rest of the world uses a more logical sequence — seventh of April, 1984.

We also had problems with meals. Sometimes we would make an appointment to come for "dinner" and arrive at 5:00 pm, only to find that "dinner" had been ready since noon. In OMF we learned to repeat the phrase, "It's not wrong, it's just different" over and over. As proud Americans we had to learn that our way wasn't "the way". No longer do we say that the Thai drive on the "wrong" side of the road or the British do it "backwards". My initial reaction to Singapore can be best expressed by the following anecdote:

Wife: "My husband and I have a strange and won-
             derful relationship."
Friend: "Oh really, how so?"
Wife: "My husband is strange and I am wonderful."

Singapore was indeed wonderful, but it was also strange. At times I'd catch myself saying, "Boy, that sure is *weird.*" But then again, "Of course it's *weird. It's supposed to be weird.*" Many of the things we encountered in Singapore seemed bizarre and uncouth, but that was all part of working in such a diverse mission as OMF.

Of the thirteen new workers six were from the United States, the rest from Canada, Malaysia, New Zealand, and South Africa. Our group contained a computer wizard, pharmacist, artist, nurse and even a street gang minister connected with the Jesus movement. Some had strong Christian backgrounds, others didn't. Our views of theology, church polity, and politics were very different. Some were Calvinistic, others not; some immersed, others sprinkled. To me, apartheid was a black and white issue of racial discrimination, but to my Afrikaans friend from South Africa it was a grey issue subject to debate. It took two months to learn to work together, agreeing to disagree on nonessentials but united in our desire to share Christ with Asians.

We were asked to speak to the young people at a Methodist Church which was celebrating its 80th anniversary. During the main service the pastor gave an altar call asking Christians to rededicate their lives. A year before, Paula and I had gone to the altar in Robesonia as an initial dedication to work in Asia. It seemed appropriate to make a further rededication of our lives now that we were on Asian soil. Hand in hand

Paula and I walked slowly to the altar rail, bowed our heads and committed the next stage of our pilgrimage into God's hands.

As we left Singapore by air for Bangkok, we realized that the excitement of courtship, engagement and honeymoon was now over. Our "marriage" to OMF was leading us to the very different environment of Bangkok.

FOUR

THE HONEYMOON ENDS

Great City of Angels, the Supreme Repository for Divine Jewels,
the Great Land Unconquerable, the Grand and Prominent Realm,
the Royal and Delightful Capital City full of Nine Noble Gems, the
Highest Royal Dwelling and Grand Palace, the Divine Shelter and
Living Place of the Reincarnated Spirits.
(Full Name of Bangkok in Thai)

The first two missionaries to touch Thai soil, Karl Gutzlaff and Jacob Tomlin, made the perilous passage from Singapore to Bangkok in 1828 aboard an old Chinese junk. It took 20 days. By plane, the same journey takes only two hours. As we stepped onto the tarmac of Don Muang Airport a blast of hot air introduced us to Bangkok, City of Angels. The city was anything but angelic, a sharp contrast to the order and efficiency of Singapore.

The base for new missionaries is a large frame house in central Bangkok called "Study House". Study House provides a smooth beginning to cultural learning for OMFers attending Union Language School (ULS). By eating in communal fashion and having laundry done for us, we were able to direct all our energies towards language learning.

Our house was located conveniently near Study House. But to get to it we had to learn to "walk the plank".

Bangkok is only one meter above sea level, and during the monsoons water stood over a foot deep around our house. Each day we had to negotiate a rickety plank set above the flood waters. In 1986 Bangkok had its worst flood ever, dumping 15 inches of water on the city in 24 hours and causing 40 deaths. It is not unusual during floods for people to step off a bus and disappear — sucked down an uncovered manhole.

When Paula first saw our house with its peeling paint and decaying eaves, surrounded by water teeming with fish, she began to cry. The kitchen was outfitted with two forks, three knives and four spoons — none of which matched. Water pressure from the tap fluctuated from a trickle to a torrent, sometimes spewing out a stream of black sludge. Paula nicknamed the house, "our jungle" due to the abundant foliage, water and wildlife.

Life in "our jungle" brought on wide fluctuations in our emotional temperature. Otherwise undetected variations in mood became magnified in such unfamiliar surroundings. Before we had never stopped to evaluate shifts in disposition or whether we were "up" or "down" on a particular day. On the homeside we greeted one another with, "How are you doing?" Here the common expression was, "How are you coping?" Taking our emotional temperature thus became a day-to-day procedure, a means of measuring how well we were handling the pressure of this new culture.

If the stress level got too high we could always count on the Study House hostess or language supervisor to lend a sensitive ear. They set up fellowship times, tutoring, and special lectures. One of the first lectures was from David Pickard, then Area Director for Thailand and now OMF's General Director Designate. He closed his talk based on Romans 1:16 with this challenge, "Never lose your confidence in the gospel." I appreciated David's timely advice. As new missionaries it was easy to lose confidence amid the various pressures and adjustments. David reminded us that God blesses His word no matter how weak the messenger.

The lectures on Thai culture were also helpful. From them I gleaned the following "Don't" list:

Don't show emotions.
Don't walk fast.
Don't point your feet.
Don't wear black or write in red.
Don't speak loudly.
Don't wear your shoes indoors.
Don't kill animals.
Don't touch anyone's head.

Our leaders knew that prayer was the lifeline of the new workers and set up daily and weekly prayer meetings for us. During the previous two years OMF had called for a worldwide prayer thrust for spiritual breakthrough in Thailand. As yet we hadn't seen such a breakthrough, but there was a note of anticipation that it wouldn't be long. I remember David Fewster, director of literature outreach, beginning a prayer with Isaiah 64:1, "Oh that you would rend the heavens and come down, that the mountains would tremble before you." Surely after 150 years of missionary work God was preparing to "rend the heavens and come down" in revival on that Buddhist nation.

It took 147 of those years for the number of churches in Bangkok to rise to fifty, but only ten more years to reach a hundred. Yet a hundred churches is so insignificant for a population of six million. My hometown in Oklahoma has almost as many churches as Bangkok, yet its population is a meager 30,000!

The church we attended was called "House of New Life". It had been started in 1974 with help from OMF and at this time had over a hundred members. Sundays are a challenge for a new worker. The tunes are familiar but you can't sing a word, or even follow the order of worship. Sermons sound like forty minutes of video run backwards. Once I listened to a sermon with pen in hand, trying to record words I knew. At the end of the sermon I had managed to write down only one word.

During our year in Bangkok we became familiar with the crowded, crooked lanes of this sprawling metropolis, with its thousands of two story shophouses, along with the occasional luxury hotel serving Thailand's billion-dollar tourist trade. Women with cropped hair and lips stained with the traditional betel nut jostled with farmers in blue homespun cloth on their way to one of the city's 200 fresh markets. On the sidewalk, uniformed students and businessmen in tailored suits pass Buddhist monks in saffron robes on their way to some of the 400 temples that dot the city. In the street, motorized rickshaws, motorbikes, taxis and buses compete for space in traffic which has been called the worst in the world.

The one-time "Venice of the East" had grown dramatically without planning or zoning laws. When OMF first surveyed Bangkok in 1951, the population was only three quarters of a million. Now it is six million, the same as Chicago but in an area half as large. Within the city limits are over a thousand slums and one million squatters. City planners expect the population to top 12 million by the year 2000.

Taxis provide the most efficient means of transportation in the city and guarantee a captive audience for sharing the gospel. Paula and I were talking with one cabby who kept referring to his life as a devout Buddhist. Suddenly, we were rammed from behind by a Peugeot sedan. Both cars stopped in the middle of a busy road while the flustered cabby negotiated with the other driver over a broken tail light. The cabby was hoping to get a large settlement for a very minor accident. The driver, however, refused to settle up and left to make a phone call. When the enraged cabby saw he wouldn't be paid, he drove forward fifteen feet and then slammed into reverse, ramming his back bumper into the grill of the Peugeot.

As we drove on I asked him to explain his beliefs to me one more time, especially the part about keeping a "cool heart".

I once read a warning outside a carnival ride, "Not recommended for pregnant women or people with heart problems." That warning should be posted on the side of every *tuk-tuk* in Bangkok. This three-wheeled, motorized pedicab is cheaper than a taxi but is so dangerous that many Thai refuse to climb into it. The driver sits like a fighter pilot in the wedged nose of his modern rickshaw, amid curling silver trim and brightly painted panels. The engine throbs with a loud erratic beat like a berserk chain saw. *Tuk-tuk* engines reach decibel levels of 120, which forces the driver to use hand signals to set the fare. Each digit on the hand represents 10 baht. *Tuk-tuk* drivers like this system because of their limited English and the fact that many are going deaf from years inside this metal loudspeaker.

When my father visited us in Thailand, he once hailed a *tuk-tuk* and asked to go to a certain hotel. The driver held up four fingers. My dad thought, *What a deal, all that way for only four baht (16 cents).* You can imagine my dad's confusion when the driver asked for 40 baht at the end of the ride!

In Thailand, the name of the game is "cram". When you buy a ticket on a Thai bus you may think you are buying a seat, but in reality you are buying a contestant fee for a telephone-booth-stuffing contest. Many public

buses in Bangkok have their frames permanently bent
due to the crush of people who congregate at the doors
or hang out by one hand.

Although language limitations closed some doors of
ministry, the Lord opened up other opportunities. When
we arrived in Thailand in 1980 there were a half million
refugees at the border. OMFer Alice Compain was visiting the Suan Plu Transit Center regularly, and asked me
to join her. What I saw was shocking. Around 600 people
were crammed into an area the size of a football field,
waiting for transfer to a third country. Thirty or forty
families sat on grass mats, each person allotted a few
square feet of space, with no partitions or privacy. The
detention section was even worse, with almost forty men
squeezed into a 20 by 40 foot cell. One leprosy patient
and four or five mentally ill shared the cell with various
criminals. Over the past months some had attempted
suicide, one by eating broken glass.

The Cambodians seemed to be the most deeply affected. From 1975 to 1979 over one million Cambodians had died under the Khmer Rouge reign of terror. A
Cambodian pastor told me that only he and his wife
survived out of an extended family of forty. Paula and I
were both sobered by this experience. Paula said, "May
I never complain to God about my circumstances again."

Out of that center Alice gathered almost twenty
Cambodians together for a Bible lesson in English which
I taught through Alice's translation. Actually, Alice could
have translated my lesson into any one of five languages.
I have a deep respect for refugee workers like her, who
help such people find not just physical refuge from
oppressive governments but spiritual refuge as well.

As a nursing mother, Paula's opportunity for ministry
was restricted. Throughout our married life Paula has
asked God to bring people to her, and He has. Her

language tutor was a petite, 24-year-old college graduate named Chutinan. Chutinan was a confirmed Buddhist, taking pride in her meditation, merit making and trips to the temple. But after a short time, she began to ask Paula questions like: "When do you pray? How long have you been a Christian? What were you like before?"

Once they were discussing hope. Paula asked, "Do you have any hope, Chutinan?"

She replied, "No, I don't."

"Do you know why I have hope?"

Chutinan answered, "Yes, because of *Phra Yesu* (the Lord Jesus)."

Paula asked finally, "What keeps you from becoming a Christian?"

"Oh, I just feel more comfortable in Buddhism and praying to Buddha."

Within a year Chutinan's attitude towards the gospel began to change. The loving concern shown by her students and many others had convinced her that Jesus was indeed the only way. Since that time her brother and sister have also trusted Christ. Chutinan's dramatic reversal reminded us once again of the power of the gospel, and of the hundreds of thousands of Chutinans here waiting for someone to lead them out of darkness into the light of the Son of God.

FIVE

A PONDEROUS BODY

*"The Thai language is like rolling a ponderous body up a steep
acclivity ... If you rest a little . . . it rolls backward."
(Dr Daniel Beach Bradley, first medical missionary to Siam)*

Our primary task during our first term was to roll that
ponderous body, the Thai language, as far up the ramp
of fluency as we could. For four years it would try our
nerves, test our patience, and consume our waking hours.
We would be misunderstood, tongue-tied and laughed
at as we tried like two year olds to form those first few
halting sentences in a new tongue. For a two year old
language is a game, but not for us. It was, in fact, the
single most important task we faced as new missionaries.
The early missionaries to Thailand were keenly aware of
this fact. The Presbyterian leaders were instructed "to
withdraw from the fields of labour any missionary who
cannot, or who does not in a reasonable time, make
himself so far master of the proper native language, as to
be understood by those who hear him."

To Hudson Taylor a "reasonable time" was only half a
year. Once he wrote home seeking new recruits for the
inland provinces of China, and assured those who volunteered that they would probably be preaching in
Chinese within six months. For missionaries to
Thailand these days a "reasonable time" is one year,

which covers formal language study in Bangkok. The next three years up-country are used to build upon the foundation laid in Bangkok.

To ensure a good foundation, we were sent to Union Language School which has small personalized classes, a good reputation, and forbids students to use English in the classroom. The first day we had to learn the school motto, *"Du dee dee, fang dee dee, khit dee dee, phud dang dang"* meaning "Look carefully, listen carefully, think carefully and speak loudly." For the next nine months we learned to look, listen and think carefully — four hours a day, five days a week.

The Thai language is akin to Chinese and was first written by King Ramkamhaeng in 1283 AD. The present script has a total of 65 characters — 44 consonants and 21 vowels. Sentences are written left to right, but without spacing between words. One must hunt for vowels since they can be found above, below, behind or in front of the consonant.

To help the new missionary, a phonetic script is used; it includes backward c's, upside down e's, an n with a tail and a crossed out u. Each day I watched my classmates strain neck muscles, roll eyeballs and thrust out their jaws in a valiant effort to utter their idea of a Thai vowel.

The tonal nature of Thai added to my frustration. English has homonyms — words that sound alike but are spelled differently and have a different meaning, like "deer" and "dear". In Thai the meaning is changed not just by spelling but by modulating the pitch of a word. For instance, the phrase *"mai mai mai mai"* with the right tones can mean "Does new silk burn?" Our teacher told us, "There are five cows (*khaw*) in Thai, but none of them give milk!"

When Paula started to study tones she knew she was in big trouble. Besides claiming to be tone deaf she had trouble divorcing her emotions from her speech. Under the pressure of a language test she tended to get excited which threw her tones into disarray. I was no expert on tones either. I have told people to *deep fry* their shoes instead of take them off, and called Samson a Nazi instead of a Nazirite.

Mistakes made by missionaries in Thai are legion — some humorous, others tragic. For instance, "Mark's gospel" and "papaya" sound similiar in Thai. You can imagine the laughs I got when I instructed a youth group to turn to Papaya's gospel, chapter 10, verse 45. The same is true of "cross" and "pants". Like other missionaries I have told Thai people that Jesus died in his pants! The following confabulation took place because "watermelon" and "marriage" sound similar in Thai.

Teacher:	"Are you *married?*"
Missionary:	"Yes, I'm a *watermelon.*"
Teacher:	"Are you sure?"
Missionary:	"Of course. I've been a *watermelon* for over ten years now."

Along a similar vein is the story of the tourist who wished to visit OMF's campsite in central Thailand, *Hang Nam* (water edge). The bus conductor, however, understood he wanted to go to *hong nam* (bathroom). At the end of the journey the conductor led him to a restroom at the terminal. The tourist then realized that he had passed his destination by sixty kilometers!

Other mistakes aren't so humorous. It is possible to call a respected elder a demon, or substitute the word "dog" for doctor. Once I asked my teacher, "Do you wash your hair?" but it came out "Do you wash me?" On another occasion I offended a Thai by inadvertently saying a cuss word. Standing over an ant hill, I began to repeat what I thought was the Thai word for "ant". A woman overheard me and in no uncertain terms let me know the nature of my error.

Once we were commenting to a neighbor on how much our son Andy's Thai had improved since attending kindergarten. The neighbor wasn't impressed. "Actually, he speaks too well, he's starting to swear in Thai." She never told us exactly what Andy was saying but one thing was for certain — the words weren't in our Thai dictionary. When Andy persisted we had to wash his mouth out with soap for words which we were still unable to define.

Blunders in language need not be all negative. Sometimes you may get an unexpected bargain. In Bangkok, you must barter with taxi drivers. A new missionary was asked by a cabby how much he was willing to pay to go to a certain hotel. The missionary meant to say "40 baht" but it came out "20 baht". The cabby replied, "Would you settle for 25?" The missionary couldn't believe his ears. A slip of the tongue saved him 15 baht!

One veteran missionary gave me this word of encouragement, "Don't worry if you are tongue-tied now. After a few years in this country you will be Thai-tongued!" Another old-timer reassured us, "You'll have no trouble learning this language, just think, 50 million people speak it fluently."

As soon as a foreigner utters a couple of words in Thai the native speaker takes it for granted that he or she is fluent and lets out a torrent of words. It is impolite to stop someone every sentence for clarification so I have developed what I call the "woodpecker wobble". The trick is to give a knowing nod at intervals as you repeat the word "krap ... krap ... krap (Is that so? Uh huh ...)" This works fine until the Thai person says something like, "Well, what do you think we ought to do in this situation?"

A new missionary does not study the Thai language in isolation. Another required course is "lessons in humility". Up country I would sometimes go with a Thai pastor to visit elderly people. Most of them had never spoken with a foreigner. Invariably the older person would ask the pastor, *"Phud dai mai?"* meaning "Can he speak?" At that point I would try to prove I could indeed speak plausible Thai. Even with that, the person would insist on using the pastor as a mediator, "Tell that foreigner that ... Ask the *farang* if he wants to ...."

Being stripped of my primary means of interacting with others was truly humbling. After twenty years of education and a Master's degree I found myself back in kindergarten. My teacher assigned a book, *500 Words to Grow On,* which was the same book we had bought for one-and-a-half-year-old Andy! Later Andy began to correct our tones and pronunciation. "No mommy, nail isn't *tabu,* it's *tapu."*

Isaiah 28:11 says, "For with stammering lips and another tongue will he speak to this people." The reference is to Assyria, yet as a language learner I identified with it, especially the part about "stammering lips". Sometimes I wondered if the stammering stage would ever end. But eventually it did, and I was able to carry on an intelligent conversation even with strangers.

A typical conversation would sound something like this:

Thai:	"How long have you been in Thailand?"
Larry:	"Three years."
Thai:	"O-O-Oh! You speak Thai very well."
Larry:	"Not really, I'm just learning."
Thai:	"Do you have a Thai wife?"
Larry:	"No, I have a foreign wife."

Thai: "Too bad. How much do you earn?"
Larry: "Enough."

The last question seems strange to westerners, but then again, we don't live in a barter economy. Almost every item is bargained for, so questions about salary or merchandise are not off limits as in the west. I have had Thai ask the price of my watch and then proceed to ask prices on almost every electrical appliance in my house.

When you meet someone in Thailand you usually don't need to remember their surname. In fact, it wasn't until 1913 that surnames were given to the Thai and to this day they relate on a first name basis. I know many Thai but the surnames of only a few.

Close friends often use nicknames. The study of nicknames is fascinating and endless. Every culture must have a Fatty, Shorty, Red, and Shrimp. But in Thailand you also find children called Fiat (automobile), Guitar, Elephant, or Talcum Powder. Nicknames are given soon after birth and usually reflect the parents' perception of the child. Our housegirl was called "Fatty" though she was skinny as a rail, while a neighbor who weighed more than I do was called "Little". In one village a man called Mosquito had a child named Elephant!

Rank and title are very important to the Thai. As a missionary I was addressed as *"Ajarn"* meaning "professor". This is hard to get used to, especially when you speak Thai on the level of a four year old. Harder still was the title *"Mo"* meaning doctor, a hangover from the early days when most missionaries practiced medicine. Sometimes I would string the Thai along claiming to be a "heart specialist". They usually listened attentively until they realized I was sharing the gospel's cure for sinful hearts. Others were convinced I was a medical doctor and would pull up their shirt and say, "Doctor, what do you think this red spot is?" Having perfected the "woodpecker wobble", I simply uttered a few *"khraps"* and advised them to return for the monthly clinic.

Friends back in the States often ask, "How long did it take you to master Thai?" After one four-year term I did feel comfortable in general conversation but I was a long way from "mastering" the language. Simply finishing a language course does not guarantee fluency; mastering a new language is a lifelong process. A Korean confirmed this for me when he said, "Foreigners need three qualities to learn Asian languages — the wisdom of Solomon, the patience of Job and the years of Methuselah."

Those who hope for immediate ministry in a foreign country will be disappointed. Once we asked a veteran nurse what advice she would give to first termers. She said, "I would have spent much more time listening and understanding the culture and people, and would have been less earnest about immediate ministry. People will forgive a first termer but are harder on a second termer who should know better."

At times we wondered if it was worth it. Did we really need to be fluent? Wouldn't a general knowledge of Thai be enough? Why did we have to spend hours making nonsense syllables, studying an incomprehensible script, and listening to tapes? But later, at a church meeting, we would realize that the point of an argument hinged on a single word.

This is why new missionaries often plead with friends back home to pray for this area of language. Paul solicited prayer support along these same lines from the Colossian Christians, "that God may *open up a door for the word*, so that we may *speak forth* the mystery of Christ, for which I have also been imprisoned; in order that I may make it *clear* in the way I ought to speak" (4:3-4).

If Paul needed clarity in making the gospel known,

how much more do new missionaries. My fear is that I will present the most meaningful message on earth in an incomprehensible manner. This is especially important in Thailand where all religions are thought to be the same, and the meaning of biblical terms is changed as they pass through the Buddhist grid. If I merely use the words *sin, salvation, heaven* and *hell* with no explanation, the Thai will draw his own conclusions and thus pervert the gospel.

Dr Bradley was right, the Thai language is a "ponderous body" and difficult to roll. Only one thing will move that body — prayer. What kind of prayer? Prayer that trusts God for open doors, boldness and clarity of speech.

SIX

PROTESTANT CEMETERY

The first duty of a soldier is obedience. The most evident duty of a soldier is to endure hardness. The ultimate duty of a soldier is to offer the supreme sacrifice. (D. M. McIntyre)

Israeli soldiers are required to visit Masada, a rocky fortress where in 73 AD, 960 Jewish defenders committed suicide rather than be captured by the Romans. For nineteen centuries Masada has been a symbol of loyalty, sacrifice and courage to the Jew. The same can be said of the monument in Washington, DC, erected in memory of soldiers who died during the Vietnam War. Americans travel from all over to read the names of some 50,000 veterans engraved in a long granite wall.

In Thailand, both Asians and foreigners make an extra effort to visit the Kanchanaburi Allied Cemetery located near the famous "Bridge over the River Kwai". This cemetery contains the remains of 6,982 of the 16,000 allies who died building the 250-mile "death railway" from Malaysia to Burma in World War II.

In Bangkok there is another war memorial, the Protestant Cemetery. In 1854 the king of Thailand donated a plot of land between the Chao Praya River and New Road for foreigners who died in Thailand. Adventurers, businessmen and officials from many nations rest side by side at this peaceful site. A large number of graves hold

the remains of missionaries who died while serving on
Thai soil. Reading their headstones is like taking a stroll
through the history of missions in Thailand. If I had my
way, I would require all new missionaries to visit it at least
once.

The engraved headstones of pioneer missionaries give
mute testimony to the heartache and adversity of those
early days. One weathered marker recorded all four
members of the Jones family who labored briefly in the
1830s. Both parents died in their thirties and their two
children survived only a few months. A high mortality
rate for both child and mother were common in those
days. In fact, the first missionary to die in Siam was Maria
Gutzlaff who expired during childbirth.

For a time the average length of service for all missionaries to Siam was less than five years. Mrs McFarland,
sailing with five other missionaries in 1860, said, "No one
in this party ever expected to see his native land again."
And no wonder. In 1859 35,000 people died of cholera
in Bangkok alone. In 1912 an epidemic of malaria and
smallpox was so bad in the north that cemeteries proved
inadequate, forcing the Thai to reclaim precious rice
fields to bury their dead. By 1927 49 career missionaries,
not counting children, had died in Thailand. By the
time OMF arrived on the scene in the early 1950's that
number had risen to over sixty.

As I stood in the cemetery I saw all around me the
silent witness of pioneer workers who established a
beachhead for Christ at great cost. These are the ones
who translated the Scriptures, distributed literature,
established schools, and opened new stations. Many of
the graves bore the initials "MD", signifying the contri-
bution that hospitals and medical workers had made to
the gospel's advance; doctors like Daniel Beach Bradley.

In the center of the cemetery is a ten-foot spire flanked

by two smaller markers. These contain the remains of Dr Bradley and his two wives. Dr Bradley arrived with his first wife in 1835. The trip from Boston to Bangkok took over a year, and they lived on salt pork, rancid butter and tepid water, enduring not only the food but a mutiny and scurvy as well. On furlough he married again, but his second wife died in Siam as well.

Dr Bradley pioneered in the area of surgery, anesthesiology, and vaccines. Later he set up a printing shop so he could distribute tracts with his medicine. The life of Dr Bradley reminded me of the grain of wheat Jesus talked about in John 12. Bradley and his wives had fallen into the still fallow soil of Siam but through their death came lasting fruit.

In the corner of the cemetery, near the river, is a small headstone which reads:

JANET ELIZABETH TOOTILL
CALLED HOME NOV 23, 1960
AGE 2 YEARS 6 MONTHS
AND JESUS CALLED A LITTLE CHILD

The name Tootill was familiar. Jim and Doreen Tootill are fellow workers who have labored in central Thailand for over 25 years. Jim had never shared with me the events surrounding the death of Janet, so I asked for details.

In November of 1960, the Tootills and their three children were traveling to Bangkok by riverboat. Near midnight, at a fork in the river, the boat capsized, throwing the family into the water. Miraculously, Doreen was able to snag their youngest, still a baby, by her dress. David, their eldest, bobbed to the surface and was rescued as well. Two-and-a-half year old Janet must have slipped by — her tiny body was found washed ashore twenty minutes later.

Working with Jim and Doreen in central Thailand is a real privilege. Jim demonstrates an unswerving confidence in the sovereignty of God, a characteristic no doubt shaped in part by Janet's death.

Close to Janet's grave is a long rectangular grey and white stone with the names of five adults and seven children engraved in a row. On the morning of January 14, 1978, a mini-van full of missionaries and their children, including two doctors and three pregnant women, was returning to the Manorom Christian Hospital after an outing. Dr Noel Sampson turned to the driver, Dr Ian Gordon-Smith, and said, "Thanks a lot Ian, it's been a beautiful morning." Ian replied lightheartedly, "We're not home yet." A few moments later, the van plowed into a six-wheel truck which was trying to pass a bus. Out of the seventeen on board, only five survived. The driver of the truck was unhurt and, as often happens, fled the scene.

We arrived two years after "the Manorom accident", as it came to be called, but repercussions were still being felt. It was sobering to meet the Juzi and Farrington families, both of whom had lost five-year-old sons in the crash. We learned that Adele Juzi, on hearing of the accident, had driven to the site hoping to help the injured, but ended up witnessing to the Thai who gathered around the crumpled van. Dr Parry had continued to work at Manorom even after losing his wife, two children and two associates in the accident. Their desire to continue serving at the hospital was a great testimony to me as a new missionary.

All the OMF graves I saw had a verse at the bottom. The Manorom grave was no exception. Next to the twelve names is Psalm 16:11, written in Thai and English:

THOU DOST SHOW ME THE PATH OF LIFE;
IN THY PRESENCE IS FULNESS OF JOY;
AT THY RIGHT HAND ARE PLEASURES
FOR EVERMORE.

Another OMFer buried in that part of the cemetery is Koos Fietje. His inscription ends with Philippians 1:21, "For me to live is Christ and to die is gain." The Fietje family had immigrated from Holland to Canada while Koos was still young. Koos worked as a baker, plumber, and metal worker before the Lord called him and his wife Colleen to Thailand in 1972.

Koos and Colleen, along with an English couple, accepted the challenge of planting a church in the town of Tatago, starting in September of 1977. Within a few months the first Thai people trusted Christ, and after a year and a half, 25 new believers were ready to be baptized. The baptismal service sparked a rash of antiChristian demonstrations, with parades planned and placards denouncing the baptisms posted up around town. The demonstrations, however, were mild compared to the reception they received at Khao Din village.

Khao Din was so far in the bush that police had little influence; a gang of ruffians controlled the area. But when a shop owner in Khao Din trusted Christ the missionaries felt a visit was in order. Koos' brother Bill, who had just joined the team, was selected to make the first visit. At first he received a grand reception, but after a while rocks began to be thrown and warning shots fired. It became increasingly dangerous to visit this "wild west" town. The missionaries had to resort to an escort in order to reduce the chance of being robbed. Koos understood the risks, but continued to nurture the new believers.

One Saturday afternoon before leaving for Khao Din, Koos told his wife, "If anything happens to me, I'm leaving my watch and ring in this drawer." He knew this next trip could be his last.

That evening around 10 pm, after the Bible study was over, Koos and a small group of believers were sipping tea and eating peanuts when a shotgun was shoved through the bamboo slats of the veranda and a single shot fired. Koos entered the presence of his Savior instantly. The date was October 24, 1981: Koos was 38 years old. Many missionaries had died in Central Thailand over the years but Koos was the first to die strictly for the gospel's sake.

Koos' death shocked the whole central Thai field, and for me as a new worker, barely two months upcountry, the impact was particularly sobering. Tatago was the first station we visited and my supervisor had at one point suggested we consider working there. I had spoken with Koos just two weeks before. Only a week before his death, Koos had said to a group of new missionaries, "We should live to live and not live to exist. It is for this reason God has created us. Today I will live to glorify God ... I will live each day as though it were my last. I am ready to go home at any time."

When I stayed in Koos' home I noticed a number of hard-backed journals along a shelf and asked about them. I was told they were a record of the Bible readings Koos had accumulated over the years. After her husband's death, Colleen explained the importance of those journals:

"Every day he would sit down with the Bible. Without any commentary, he would read from the Scripture and make notes. He did this the whole first term we were in Thailand, from Genesis to Revelation and starting in Genesis again. Through this he became a changed person. I believe the Lord has been able to use him more in the last years of his life than when we first went to Thailand, because he knew God's Word, and was able to share it with others."

The Word of God had transformed Koos and his ministry. One senior missionary commented that Koos lived more closely with the Thai than any other missionary he knew. Koos believed you had to win the Thai to yourself first before you could win them to Christ. "The Christ that the Thai see is you and me," he would say. "We must be a living example of the truth we preach."

Three months after the earth was turned over Koos' grave, the OMF family found itself once again at the Protestant Cemetery, this time mourning the death of a child. Near Koos' grave is a small marker with faded letters which reads:

CHRISTOPHER IAN ELLARD
DIED JAN 15, 1982 AGE 9
SAFE IN THE ARMS OF JESUS

Chris was the son of Alan and Maelyn Ellard who had served as our supervisors during language study in Bangkok. Chris and his twin brother would often catch fish with nets under our house. One day he was climbing in an attic when the ceiling gave way. As he fell, his head struck the floor, knocking him unconscious. On January 12 we got word that he was in the hospital on a respirator; he died three days later.

As with the Manorom accident, it wasn't just adults who grieved. Chris had many friends in Thailand and at boarding school in Malaysia. Losing Chris was like losing a close family member.

As a new worker, these deaths reminded me of the cost that church planters are sometimes asked to pay in order to see the Kingdom advanced. In the thirty years since OMF's work began in Thailand, 22 members of the mission had died violently, some in accidents, others martyred. Yet in a sense we were only following in the steps of the China Inland Mission. During the Boxer Rebellion of 1900, 58 CIMers were martyred along with 21 children. Hudson Taylor wrote to those on the field then, "It is a wonderful honour He has put upon us as a mission to be trusted with so great a trial, and to have among us so many counted worthy of a martyr's crown."

In Hebrews 11 there is an honor roll of saints who, like good soldiers, were willing to endure hardship. At the Protestant Cemetery I saw another honor roll, this one written in stone. The blood of those on that honor roll was becoming the seed of the church. Their deaths were not in vain.

The son of Adoniram Judson wrote, "If we succeed without suffering, it is because others have suffered before us. If we suffer without success, it is that others may succeed after us." J.O. Sanders adds this note, "God does not waste suffering, nor does He discipline out of caprice. If He plow, it is because He purposes a crop."

In the *seminary* classroom I was taught many principles of church growth. The *cemetery* classroom, however, taught me a lesson seldom touched upon in church growth classes — the principle of death. Jesus said in John 12: 24, "... unless a grain of wheat falls into the earth and *dies*, it bears much fruit." Much grain has been sown in Thai soil over the past 160 years. These deaths have not been wasted. God is simply sowing seed for a greater harvest which many feel is right on the horizon.

SEVEN

MECCA OF BUDDHISM

In a social sense, a man cannot be born, educated, married, build a house, recover from an illness, plant and harvest a crop, or die without some practice prescribed by his religion. It is a social as well as religious system, so the Thai embracing Christianity finds himself ostracized from his native society. (Carl Zimmerman)

When Paul visited Athens, the book of Acts records that, "his spirit was *stirred in him,* when he saw the city wholly given to idolatry." The adoration of Greek gods produced a visceral reaction deep within Paul's spirit. At first I sensed a similar stirring when confronted with the pervasive idolatry found in Thailand. As time passed, however, idols of stone and wood became so familiar and commonplace that I began to lose that sense of righteous indignation so evident in Paul.

A turning point occurred on a trip with another OMFer to a cave. Inside were the typical assortment of statues, shrines and altars found at almost all tourist sites. I invited my friend to explore the cave with me, but he adamantly refused even to set foot inside. He reminded me that idolatry was an affront to a Holy God who "is angry with the wicked every day" (Psalm 7:11 KJV). It was then I realized how desensitized one can become to the idolatry so evident in Thailand's major religion — Buddhism.

Buddhism was brought to Thailand in the 13th century by monks from Sri Lanka. It began to take root and was soon absorbed into the local animistic religion. When the first Christian missionaries arrived in the 1830s, Buddhism was well established as the national religion, dominating the Thai psyche, thought patterns, and culture. Early missionaries found this fortress of Buddhism virtually impregnable. Dr Daniel Bradley described the Thai as "spiritual marble statues". The Presbyterians labored nineteen years before baptizing their first convert. J.E. Meakin gave this analysis in 1886, "I believe there is no country more open to unrestrained missionary effort than Siam, but I believe that there can hardly be a country in which it is harder to make an impression." Take their understanding of John 3:16, for instance. This famous verse, run through the Buddhist grid, presents a very confused picture of Christianity:

"For *God* (Buddhism has no concept of a creator God) ... so *loved* (a desire to be quenched)... the *world* (an illusion) ... that He *gave* (giving is done in order to get, repayment is expected) ... His only begotten *Son* (this God has a wife?) ... that whoever *believes in Him* (Buddha said, 'Be a lamp unto yourself,' and 'work out your own salvation with diligence.') ... should not *perish* (hell is not eternal separation but temporary) ... but have *eternal life* (the goal of Buddhism is nirvana — the extinction of suffering and the end of conscious existence)."

In fact, the whole of John 3 presents problems for the Thai. Take being born again. The last thing a Thai wants to do is be reborn. As a believer in reincarnation, his goal is to stop the never-ending cycle of birth/old age/sickness/death. The Thai equate rebirth not with spiritual renewal but with suffering.

Invariably, when you share Christ with the Thai you

run into semantic problems. It is possible to talk for hours with a Buddhist, stressing the exclusiveness of the Christian message and Christ's claim of being the only way to God. Yet at the end of the conversation a Thai will conclude, "All religions are the same, they teach us to be good people."

Apologetics and logic don't work either. A Thai university professor was confronted with the argument that Jesus was either Lunatic, Liar or Lord — logic demands a choice be made between these three options. The professor's syncretistic mind was able to defy logic and thus offer this answer, "Jesus was 10% Lunatic, 20% Liar and 70% Lord."

Many Christian concepts fly right in the face of what the Thai have been taught from an early age. In 1939 the name of the country was officially changed from Siam to Thai (free) land. The Thai, who take pride in their freedom, cannot accept the idea of Jesus being Lord, and Christians His slaves. I have heard monks on the radio warn people, "Don't become a slave of Jesus, otherwise you will lose your Thainess."

Galatians 6:7 says that what you sow you will reap, but the law of *karma* is the opposite, "What a man reaps, that he has sown in a previous life". Christianity promises forgiveness, but Buddha said, "Man cannot be freed from an evil deed." Buddhism teaches that man is born innocent and only sins when a law is broken, while the Bible maintains that all men are born in sin and can sin even in their thought life.

Nowhere is the contrast clearer than when you compare the purpose of life in each system. Buddhism is basically fatalistic. The Buddhist views himself as an actor in a play, with the script already determined by his deeds or misdeeds from a previous life. This fatalistic mindset probably explains the casual Thai attitude to

life. One missionary observed a gasoline station on fire,
with the flames spreading towards a large tank. She
watched in amazement as the attendant calmly filled his
bucket and threw it on the flames, then leisurely walked
back to fill his bucket again. You can see the same thing
in the notorious traffic jams in Bangkok. In the west,
horns would be honked and tempers vented, but the
Thai sit patiently and quietly until the traffic untangles.
The Thai have been called "masters of unconcern" and
one of the first phrases a foreigner learns is *mai pen rai*
(never mind, it doesn't matter).

After a while this *mai pen rai* attitude begins to affect
even the most fastidious westerner. As a new missionary
I avoided ice, unboiled water and food from street vendors, having been warned of the health hazards. The
lane on which we lived, however, had a number of carts
laden with Thai delicacies. The aroma of barbequed
sausage, sauté pork, corn on the cob and fried chicken
began to win out. Finally I whispered *mai pen rai* under
my breath, sat down and ordered my first meal off the
street.

Over 200,000 Buddhist monks live in almost 30,000
temples scattered around Thailand.   Almost all Thai
men enter the monkhood for a period of time — a few
days, the three months of Buddhist Lent or a number of
years. In the pale light of early morning you can see
saffron-colored figures emerging from narrow lanes,
barefoot and carrying a brass alms bowl to receive food
from devout Thai who thereby earn merit. Temple
attendants trail dutifully behind with extra containers in
hand. A housewife removes her shoes and then gives a
graceful bow as she places plastic bags of curry, rice or
sweet meats in the monk's bowl. The monk accepts the
gift without any indication of thanks; to show appreciation would take away merit from the offerer.

A monk starts his day at 3:30 am and begs food between 5:30 and 7:00 am. He lives an ascetic life in a small
cubicle, free of material possessions, practicing meditation, studying the Buddhist scriptures, and eating only
two meals a day. He must not steal, lie, talk idly, take life,
indulge in sex or luxuries — 227 rules govern his every
moment. He can have no possessions except the yellow
robe, the alms bowl, and a few personal necessities.

As Paula entered a bus one day, she noticed that the
only unoccupied seat was next to a monk. As she made
her way innocently to the spot, a number of Thai men
switched places, thus ensuring that she was seated well
clear of the monk. Later she learned that one of the 227
rules forbids a monk even to touch a woman.

At first I diligently studied the doctrines of Buddhism
in order to relate to the Thai. I now know that there is
no such thing as "pure" Buddhism in Thailand, it is a
curious mixture of Hinduism, Brahmanism and folk
religion. "Syncretistic folk Buddhism," says Alex Smith,
"is like a sponge which sucks up new ideas and conforms
them suitably to itself without making any perceivable
change in the sponge." [1] That is why it is not difficult to
get Thai people to "profess faith" in Christ. Many see no
problem in believing in Jesus and Buddha at the same
time. In major hotels in Bangkok you can find *The
Teachings of Buddha* alongside a Gideon Bible. It is not
unusual to find Bible correspondence courses stacked
next to a Buddhist altar.

Once we hosted 25 students from Hong Kong who
came to do evangelism in the town where we were living.
Since they spoke no Thai, they simply had the person
read from the Four Spiritual Laws booklet. If the person

[1] *Siamese Gold*

smiled at the end, the student would bring them to me so I could "lead them to Christ". When I asked more pointed questions it was obvious that they were just being polite, listening with apparent interest but with no real intention to break with the past.

Buddhism in Thailand is like a pie. The crust is theoretical Buddhism but beneath the crust is a complex world of Hindu gods, astrology, magical charms and venerated spirits. It is the spirit world which holds the real power and as such must be revered, feared, and placated.

To gain protection from the spirits or to insure physical safety most Thai wear amulets around their neck or waist. These magical charms often consist of a clay tablet with an impression of the Buddha, encased in plastic and hanging by a gold chain. Every village has a merchant who "rents" them, and it is not unusual to see men around a park bench trading them like postage stamps. They come in five colors, the most powerful being black, which they claim can protect the wearer from car accidents, gunfire and snakebite, or increase fertility. I've even seen Buddhists wearing a cross. Once I asked a group of Thai if they would come to church. They asked, "Do we get a free cross?" To them a cross is not just a symbol but a Christian amulet, and as such should bring good fortune as well as protection.

The Thai also rely on spirit houses for protection. Early in the morning you can see barefoot men and women kneeling before a miniature house, their palms pressed together and their eyes closed. As incense and jasmine are placed on the shelf a prayer is made for a good harvest, a lottery number, or the safe birth of a grandchild. Almost every house and business has such a house on its property. Sometimes it is simply a rusty tin can, other times it is an elaborate mini-temple beside a luxury hotel. Resident spirits are said to have powers to bless or plague the inhabitants. They must be placated by offerings of food, fresh flowers and incense.

Possibly the most famous shrine is on the grounds of the former Erawan Hotel in Bangkok. Before completion of the hotel in 1956 there were a number of mysterious accidents. An expert on the occult suggested a shrine to the Hindu god Shiva be erected. Accidents suddenly decreased and the reputation of the shrine spread. Young couples hoping for a child and those seeking the national lottery prize are frequent visitors. A crowd of police, dancers, merchants, and worshipers can be seen there around the clock. So famous is this shrine that Caesar's Palace in Las Vegas had a replica imported from Thailand.

The Temple of the Emerald Buddha is even more venerated than Erawan. The Thai regard it as their most holy place, and every Thai tries to visit the site at least once in his lifetime. It houses a three-foot jade Buddha, a prototype of millions of such images which inundate the land. Buddha images come seated, standing and reclining in every shape, size and color. Government seals, flags and coins often bear Buddhist images. Rings, pendants, and necklaces constantly remind you of the pervasive presence of Gautama Buddha.

Exposure to idolatry in the east helped unearth a subtle form of idolatry in my own heart. Idolatry doesn't need to be tied to images of stone or wood but can be anything that replaces God in our life or robs God of His glory. In the west it is most often seen in the form of materialism. I had never offered incense to a sports car or bowed before a newly purchased computer, yet my concern and anxiety over such material things was just as culpable as the blatant idolatry I saw in Thailand.

I also learned that the cure for idolatry is always costly.

When a Thai breaks with the spirits or his previous religion he must count the cost both financially and spiritually. Idols are often very expensive and are passed from generation to generation. To destroy such heirlooms often brings ostracism and persecution from family members. Yet for the Christian there is no alternative. All idols, whether images or material objects, must be shattered if victory is to be achieved.

EIGHT

GREENHORNS AND TENDERFOOTS

*Making disciples takes time. It cannot be done through a series of
lectures and a training seminar in the church,
nor can it be done by reading a book. It cannot be rushed...
Disciples are made, but not mass produced. Each one is molded and
fashioned individually by the Spirit of God..*
(Walter Henrichsen)

Thailand is divided into two basic areas: Bangkok (civilization) and upcountry (everywhere else). After four months our supervisor said, "Larry, it's time you went *upcountry*." What he meant was, "We've nursed you long enough. It's time you got out of the nest (study house) and learned to fly on your own." Our first "upcountry" trip was to a thirty-bed OMF hospital in a village called Nongbua in Central Thailand.

After hours of travel by bus, taxi and rickshaw we were greeted by Dr Graham and Heather Roberts from England, our hosts for two weeks. I asked Dr Roberts' colleague, Dr Ursie Lowenthal, if it would be possible to see some surgery during my stay. She replied, "Sure, I'll call you when we get something 'interesting'."

A few nights later I received a call from Dr Ursie. "Larry, I've finally got something *interesting* — a knifing." I had never seen surgery before and would have been happy with hangnail or corn removal. Evidently Ursie thought differently.

As I entered the operating theater, I saw her fever-ishly working on a young man named Cheway. She had sawn his sternum in two and was prying his rib cage apart with a metal instrument. Dr Ursie fought valiantly to save Cheway's life, but three days later he was dead. I can still see his teenage wife sitting with her head bowed, staring blankly into space, unresponsive to both relatives and hospital staff. To me she was a graphic picture of the despair and hopelessness that Thai people feel in the face of the ultimate reality — death.

At Nongbua, the doctors didn't have access to sophis-ticated equipment like fetal monitors, CAT scans or special drugs. Often they improvised. Once I saw Dr Roberts poring over a manual, and asked, "Why are you so intent on that book?"

He replied, "I'm scheduled to do eye surgery in a few minutes."

"Is it going to be a complicated surgery?"

"I'm not sure; I've never done it before," was his casual reply.

Later that week Dr Roberts had an "interesting" case of his own for me to witness — a gunshot victim. A young man had accidentally shot himself at close range in the forearm. After that experience I decided to forego any more "interesting" cases and concentrate on church work instead.

Jan Poot, from Holland, had helped plant a church in Nongbua. He agreed to take me on his Honda 90 to visit church members and follow up contacts. The first visit was to the home of an eighty-year-old shut-in woman. Before entering the house Jan found a large stick which he carried at ready before him. I wondered why a club was necessary — it didn't seem very neighborly.

I asked, "Why the stick, Jan?"

He said, "You'll find out."

At that moment two ferocious dogs leaped from under the house. Ever since that visit I have included a club as standard equipment for "up-country" visitation.

Although poor and in bad health, our shut-in still maintained a sense of humor. Evidently Jan's Scripture readings and songs were too slow for this octogenarian, so she broke in, "You'd better hurry up your singing and praying, sonny. I may die before you finish!"

A little further down the road Jan stopped by a rice field so I could try my hand at harvesting rice. On my first few attempts I couldn't even get my sickle to cut the stalks. The farmer instructing me asked, "What's rice like in the United States?"

I said, "I don't know, I've never seen any growing before. We get ours out of a box."

"A box?" the farmer replied wih a puzzled look.

I got an equally puzzled look the time I tried to plant rice seedlings in a paddy field. My teacher demonstrated how to push the seedlings into the mud in a set pattern, then he left me on my own for a while. When he returned, the carefully laid rice plot was in disarray — half of the seedlings I had "planted" were floating on the surface of the water!

Finally, I got an easy assignment. Heather Roberts told me how to order a certain cut of pork from the Thai butcher for our Christmas dinner. Heather didn't say anything when I returned from the butcher but at our Christmas meal I noticed the meat was a bit tough. Only later did Heather inform me of my error — I had ordered water buffalo, not pork. Needless to say, she didn't send me on any more errands.

Our second "up-country" trip took place in March, the hottest month of the year. We spent two weeks with another Roberts family — Ian and Maybeth from New Zealand. They were starting a church in Khoksamrong, a town of 11,000 people in central Thailand. Their residence, called House of New Life, was like a warehouse, with unfinished walls, exposed wiring and a large sliding metal door. The Roberts' simple lifestyle gave them ready access to merchants and vendors on their lane. Like Paul, they were becoming all things to all men that they might win some. They had even adopted a ten-year-old girl named "Bird" who had been rejected by her parents when she confessed Christ.

Our first day with the Roberts in Khoksamrong went very smoothly — until night fell.

After the lights were out I noticed a buzzing in my ear that got louder and louder. We had spread a mosquito net, so I knew that couldn't be the problem, but the buzzing persisted. Finally, Paula and I realized our net was indeed teeming with mosquitos. I tried to blow them away with a ceiling fan, but the heavy netting kept out the wind. Hiding under the covers was out unless you didn't mind heat stroke. Outside the covers you risked becoming a human pincushion. Beneath our window a night watchman beat a gong every hour on the hour throughout the night. We heard every one!

The next morning we stumbled, red-eyed and groggy, to the breakfast table. Maybeth asked innocently, "How did you sleep?"

Paula replied, "Terrible, we were eaten alive by mosquitos."

Ian replied, "You did remember to tuck in the mosquito net, didn't you ...?"

During the five years that Ian had lived in Khoksamrong there had never been a Christian funeral. In a five-day period during our stay there were two. The first was a young mother of three, who had been struck by a stray bullet when two men quarreled at an outdoor movie. Five days later, a man with cancer died in another village. I'll never forget how non-Christian relatives fired pistols at the cremation site in order to scare away the spirits.

At one point during the long service Paula asked in her best Thai, *"Hong nam yu thi nai?* — where is the bathroom?"* The hostess seemed puzzled by her question. Paula tried again, *"Hong nam yu thi nai?"* Another blank stare. Paula tried to describe it, "You know, little room ... with hole in floor ..."

The hostess finally caught on, "Oh, you mean a bathroom: we don't have one."

Exasperated, Paula asked, "Then what should I do?"

The woman pointed to an adjacent field, "Pick a bush, any bush."

Paula wrote later, "My missionary blood being quite thin, I decided to wait until we got home."

Our two "upcountry" experiences reminded us just how inexperienced we were as missionaries. Oklahomans use two terms to describe the likes of us, "tenderfoots" and "greenhorns". A tenderfoot is a newcomer who has yet to be hardened to frontier life. A greenhorn was described by a cowboy as "a man who couldn't cut a lame steer from a tree." As both tender and green missionaries we knew it was going to take years to adjust to Thai manners and customs. Paula decided that missionaries are made, not born. Language study and lectures in Bangkok were fine, but one day we would need to test out that theory in an "upcountry" situation.

We swore, however, that if we moved upcountry we would never live in a house like the House of New Life. That was fine for the Roberts, but not for us. God must have a sense of humor, because when we received our designation for our second term it was — House of New Life, Khoksamrong!

At the end of our first year in Bangkok the reality of

missionary service began to sink in. Gone was the excitement of exotic Singapore. Gone too was the romantic euphoria of those first few weeks in Bangkok. No longer would we have the luxury of supermarkets, malls, and McDonalds. No longer would we study Thai in an air-conditioned classroom, eat communally and play volleyball in the afternoon. We were designated to central Thailand, a vast area with few conveniences or comforts and a struggling church made up mostly of leprosy patients. The honeymoon was definitely over.

NINE

DARK PLACES OF THE EARTH

I know that I have opportunities of usefulness at home;
nevertheless, in heathen lands there is gross darkness
and scarely any gleam of light.
(Thomas Ragland)

... the dark places of the earth are full of the habitations of cruelty.
(Psalm 74:20)

Sometimes you hear stories of missionaries who locate a primitive tribe, evangelize and plant a church without any outside assistance. Our ministry, however, was not done in a vacuum. It was the culmination of thirty years of trail-blazing by other OMFers.

The last missionaries of the China Inland Mission were still straggling out of China in 1951 as the first missionary arrived in Bangkok. The policy of the mission had always been to give priority to unreached areas. Since no Thai churches existed in the vast rice basin of central Thailand, a survey team was sent there to make a feasibility study.

Reading about this initial survey trip reminded me of the conquest of Canaan. The central provinces, like Canaan, were spacious and fruitful, covered with vast seas of rice and abundant water. The interpreter for the "spies" was Emerson Frey, who qualified for the job

because he had been in the country six whole weeks!
Like Joshua and Caleb, the team brought back a positive
report. The thirteen provinces were a good prospect for
pioneer church planting. This 24,000-square-mile area
of paddy fields and rocky wooded hills along with two
million inhabitants, had been bypassed by other mission
groups and was virtually untouched for Christ.

This area, once called "the missionary graveyard", was
truly one of "the dark places of the earth." The "spies"
observed many leprosy sufferers but failed to find even
one hospital. It was true there were giants in the land,
yet this tiny band believed that the "shout of faith" could
bring down even the strongest barriers. Their recom-
mendation was first to send a medico-evangelistic launch
down the waterways, and later to start a hospital.

The missionaries pouring out of China to Thailand
wanted to spread the gospel as quickly and widely as
possible. They believed in the domino theory: China
had just fallen to the communists and Thailand was
likely to be next. They would never have imagined that
35 years later the domino would still be standing.

After the boat ministry, strategy shifted to more per-
manent stations located in major towns. One was Lopburi,
154 kilometers north of Bangkok. Lopburi had waited
290 years for a gospel witness; the last missionaries there
were Jesuit priests who arrived in 1665. Close on their
heels came a Greek explorer, Constantine Phaulkon.
Constantine became friends with the ruler of Thailand,
King Narai, who asked the Greek to accompany him to
Lopburi. Phaulkon picked up the Thai language in only
two years and became a trusted advisor to the king.

Phaulkon asked the king to supply land and materials
to build a chapel. The king complied. His officials,
however, resented the Catholic presence as well as the
lavish European lifestyle of King Narai's "Greek favo-

rite". When the king lay ill in 1688, one of his brothers seized the throne and arrested Phaulkon for treason. When he was beheaded on June 5, 1688 the flicker of the gospel was extinguished.

Once I toured the extensive ruins of King Narai's royal palace and the equally impressive palace of Phaulkon. These palaces dominate the center of town with their massive three-foot-thick walls and high battlements. Near the main temple are elephant stables, as well as a building with gothic windows — the chapel in Phaulkon's day.

I asked the curator of the museum if there were any relics the Catholics might have left behind. He took me through some dusty corridors to a small room, on the wall of which were a foot-high silver cross and a set of silver candelabras. As I examined these relics I began to think of the irony of it all. In 1688 the candles in those candelabras had been yanked out and replaced by incense and the yellow tallow candles of Buddhism. Since that time the cross, and the Savior it represents, had been relegated to a back room.

Constantine Phaulkon helped bring the gospel to Lopburi as an ambassador for the French government, but his mission had failed. OMFers Em and Grace Frey had come to Lopburi as ambassadors for the King of Kings, and their mission was destined to succeed. God was once again giving a chance for the light of the gospel to burn in Lopburi.

To plant the gospel in one of the oldest Buddhist centers in Thailand was a formidable task. Temples dominate the landscape and ruins spanning over twelve centuries can still be seen. The symbol of Lopburi is a thirteenth century laterite-block shrine called "Sacred Three Spires". Every time I use a 500 baht note with its picture of those three spires, I am reminded of the shrine's influence. Next to it is the "monkey temple" where monkeys freely roam the grounds and are fed by the worshipers. A few kilometers from Lopburi is the Footprint of Buddha Temple, which was once considered a center of pilgrimage for Buddhists the world over.

Buddhism was deeply entrenched in this provincial capital. The people's devotion was best seen at the palace, where hundreds of headless Buddha figures stood along the corridors. The Burmese had decapitated these idols centuries before but the Thai still preserved and worshiped them. The influence of Buddhism and superstition radiated out from Lopburi city like so many tentacles to the 600,000 inhabitants of the province.

At the famous winter fair in Lopburi I saw with my own eyes the pervasive influence of Buddhism. That year local Christians had set up a booth from which to distribute 100,000 Scripture portions. The paths were white with discarded tracts, as people ground underfoot the precious seed of God's Word. Yet, as in the parable, not all seed falls on the path; some is bound to fall on good soil. One such person was a Chinese merchant named Mrs Saijai. Her first husband had left her, and one day she was on her way to draw water when she heard a missionary preaching in the market. She longed to hear more, and after a month she believed. She was baptized on Easter Day, 1956. Later she had a short-lived marriage to a drunken boxer, but her faith held firm. It was still firm 25 years later. In fact it was Mrs Saijai who played a pivotal role in helping us plant a church.

Once there was a bad fire in the area of Lopburi where the missionaries lived. The landlord's house right next door was burning, and the eaves of their house caught fire. Cyril Faulkner threw water on them through the upstairs windows, which saved the house. He carried most of his earthly goods onto the street, and Mrs Saijai sat and watched them throughout the rest of the night while he worked to protect the house. Though poor, she would not take any renumeration.

Emerson and Grace Frey were the first to explore the province, using the provincial city as a base. One town they were interested in, about ninety kilometers to the northeast, was called Lamnarai. Em Frey recalls stopping at a village which fascinated his children, with its huge temple and swinging bridge over a deep chasm. Lamnarai was not so fascinating. "Lamnarai was just two rows of dull grey wooden shops with farm equipment, supplies, and carts all over the brown dirt street," he told us.

Once the Freys hitched a ride to Lamnarai on a soft drink truck. For ninety bumpy kilometers they endured the only available seat — a wooden coke case. On arrival at the market the Freys would rent a shop, give out tracts and preach from posters. Sometimes they brought their own snacks, but existed mainly on noodles and bottled drinks.

A welcome change from the coke truck was the Gospel Rover, which was used for film showings in and around Lamnarai. In the evening a screen, projector, book table, and generator were set up in the temple grounds. Such film showings brought large crowds who stayed throughout the program, even when the generator failed.

Another outreach in Lamnarai was a monthly leprosy clinic held in a tiny pavilion on the property of a Christian with leprosy, Mr Hit. The Freys went along with the nurses to preach to patients and train the Christians. By visiting this and other clinics, they were able to locate over thirty Christians in the province.

As transportation improved a number of these Christians began to meet one Sunday a month at the leprosy clinic in Lopburi city for worship. Social barriers between "well" and leprosy Christians caused them to meet separately for many years, but gradually a few "well" Christians broke rank to visit the leprosy group. Ratana, a hairdresser, was the first to step over the line. It was hard for new Christians like Ratana to eat with their leprosy brothers and sisters, but eventually prejudices began to crumble and the groups came together.

In 1973, Ian and Maybeth Roberts from New Zealand arrived to help the Freys in Lopburi. Ian preferred a motorcycle to a Land Rover, and once a month he took Mr Hit on a one or two day tour of the virgin territory around Lamnarai. Travel by motorcycle was difficult no matter what season. In the dry season, Ian was choked by dust as he drove along the deeply rutted trails. After one particularly bumpy ride he grabbed for a box of aspirin. When he opened it, fifty percent of the medicine had been reduced to powder.

Once Ian made a ten-kilometer trip in less than a half hour on a dry gravel road. During his visit it rained, making the return trip five hours long! At two places he had to cross deep chasms. One had a suspension bridge barely wide enough to drive across, and the other was crossed by a cable system in which the cycle was placed in a wooden box and pulled across.

The persistant efforts of Ian, Mr Hit and others began to bear fruit. In 1978 missionaries started holding weekly meetings in Lamnarai to help nurture the handful of believers.

When the Assyrians attacked Israel in 722 BC they devastated the land and scattered the people. Seven centuries later at the time of Christ, that area was still considered a "burned over" district by the populace. This picture changed, however, when Jesus made his momentous trip north to Galilee. Matthew 4:16 says, "The people living in darkness have seen a great light, on those living in the land of the shadow of death a light has dawned."

Central Thailand was the Galilee of Thailand. For over a hundred years the church bypassed these thirteen spiritually dark and backward provinces. Lopburi, a center of pagan religions for centuries, was one of the darkest. In the 1670's a dim light flickered for a time but was extinguished. Three centuries later, that flicker of light was rekindled by the arrival of the Freys. By the 1970s the Lopburi city church had become a steady flame. However, large pockets of darkness remained in the province. One of them was the area around Lamnarai.

TEN

CHURCH PLANTING 101

From the beginning, expect to plant a church your first term.
(Robert Erion, OMFer working in South Thailand)

Nirut, a young Thai pastor, had made the 500-kilometer bus ride from his home province in north-east Thailand to Bangkok numerous times. Through the dust-caked bus window he could see villages and market towns spread out like so many chess-pieces over the checkered rice fields of the central plain. One of those market towns was Lamnarai. Set back from the main road, it was not much more than two rows of shop-houses along a single thoroughfare. Like hundreds of similiar towns along the route, it was in spiritual darkness. Each trip brought an increasing burden on Nirut's heart. He longed to see churches spring up all along that important highway, but in 1972 there was not even one.

That same year Nirut accepted a call to pastor a church in Bangkok. Although caught up in the activities of a large urban church, he did not forget his initial burden for the towns along the highway. In 1974, during the dry season, he led a team of ten Thai to evangelize the Lamnarai market. Although they ministered only two days, they were encouraged by the response and left two team members behind to do follow-up. Six months later he took a larger group including a Canadian missionary, set up a stage in front of the police station and began a nightly preaching/healing service. A loudspeaker summoned those who desired to be healed. Word of the meetings spread rapidly and people from surrounding villages began to attend.

Up to this point the team had met little opposition. They were viewed more as a curiosity than a threat. As the week wore on, however, that scene changed. The meetings often lasted past midnight. When those from distant villages realized they couldn't return home they became upset, and rocks were thrown. The team's insistance that a man remove his amulet caused even more agitation.

Finally a gang of ruffians disrupted the meetings, mounting the stage to hit and kick the team members. The missionary, badly beaten, was quickly carried to safety. Eventually the police arrived to quell the riot. Churches in Thailand are often born in adversity; Lamnarai was no different.

Even with this setback, Pastor Nirut was determined to see a church started. He sent a young preacher to hold weekly meetings in a rented house in the market. One of those early contacts was Auntie Tam.

God had miraculously prepared Auntie Tam's heart. One night ten luminous figures holding books appeared alongside her bed. Fifteen days later Nirut's evangelistic team arrived in Lamnarai. The team members were the same people Tam had seen in her vision and they carried Bibles! Although poor herself, Tam entertained the evangelistic team like royalty, watching after their needs and preparing food. Her notorious husband, Chan, couldn't care less. Chan had built a reputation as a drunkard with numerous minor wives, and viewed Christians with contempt.

Unfortunately, meetings for Tam and the other new

Christians lasted only a year and a half. The young pastor evidently ran away with a woman who was attending the meetings. Sporadic visits to Lamnarai by OMF missionaries over the next few years barely held the small group of believers together. Resident missionaries were needed, who could give themselves totally to church planting. That opportunity finally came in 1981.

Our family was nearing the end of language school but was still uncertain where we would be working. We longed to be discipled by a senior couple in an established church; but no senior workers were available. Buzz and Ruthi Curtis faced the same dilemma. As Buzz and I talked, we decided it would be better to have two "greenhorn" couples together in a new station than to end up somewhere alone with no coworker. We realized that in many situations we would be merely "pooling our ignorance", but it seemed worth the risk.

Buzz and I compiled a list of ten reasons why we felt our families should work together, and submitted it to the Area Director. Our request was granted; we would be the first resident missionaries to live in Lamnarai.

David Pickard, the Area Director, gave a final admonition to those of us planning to move up-country. It consisted of six pithy exhortations:

1. Fear God and you need not fear man.
2. Never lose your confidence in the gospel.
3. Believe God.
4. Be ready to preach, pray, or die at a moment's notice.
5. It is an honor to suffer dishonor, disgrace, or discomfort for His sake.
6. Learn to look at each situation from God's perspective.

Another exhortation I never forgot was from Robert Erion, who in his first term planted a church from scratch in Betong on the Thai-Malaysia border. When Robert learned I was going to a new station, he said, "Expect to plant a church your first term."

I wanted to say, "What do you mean 'plant a church'? I've yet to plant the Thai language in my brain, and have a long way to go with Thai culture and beliefs." Upon reflection, however, Robert's words were just what I needed. Instead of living the next three years defensively — trying to fulfill mission obligations and merely surviving — I needed to, as William Carey said, "expect great things from God, attempt great things for God." To set our sights any lower would be to question God.

For its first 25 years of work in central Thailand the mission concentrated on rural areas, apart from a few major towns. In 1979 the strategy was changed to include district or *amphur* towns which have a population of 4,000 to 100,000 people and are the administrative and economic centers of the district. OMF set a goal of having a 25-member church in all 65 *amphurs* in Central Thailand by 2003 (the 50th anniversary of OMF work there). When we finished our term 23 *amphurs* had churches, leaving 42 without any resident witness.

Lamnarai was one such *amphur.* Robert Erion had advised me to "keep contact with the upper crust but concentrate on the common people." Living in an *amphur* town would allow us to meet wealthy merchants and officials and yet minister to farmers and leprosy patients.

On August 31, 1981, we boarded a bus for Lamnarai, travelling the same route Pastor Nirut had used ten years before. We were full of anticipation. 1981 was sandwiched between two great events: the 1978 commemoration of 150 years of mission work in Siam, and the 1982 Bicentenniel celebration of Thailand itself. The years 1978-79 had been devoted to prayer for breakthrough in Thailand. Surely a revival was on its way — would it start in Lamnarai?

The bus took us from Bangkok to a level plain covered with a vast sea of rice. As we neared our destination the scenery changed to a rolling plateau. The town itself was located on the crossroads of two major arteries, and had a population of 10,000.

After unpacking our barrels and getting the house into order, I had time to reflect on the magnitude of our task. Our goal was to "plant a church", but what did that actually entail? The seed of God's Word had been faithfully sown in this area for many years. I hoped for a repetition of John 4:37, "One sows, and another reaps." Possibly God would allow us to be in the group of reapers.

People at home considered us pioneers. I rather liked the title. Before arriving in Lamnarai I even began to fancy myself as such a trail blazer, cutting a swath through heathen territory for the gospel's sake. I quickly realized, however, that planting a church was not going to be as glamorous or attractive as the missionary biographies I had read on the homeside. The root word for pioneer is actually *peon* — a common footsoldier, a subordinate, a slave. Planting a church was going to be plain hard work, a lonely and often discouraging task more suited to privates than generals.

At that time I felt much more like a buck private than a commanding general. Possibly Solomon's emotions before the erection of the temple best fit mine. "My son Solomon ... is *still young* and *inexperienced* and the *work is great* ..." (I Chronicles 29:1). How were four young and inexperienced workers going to plant a viable church in only three years?

Our homes, which stood side by side, were identical: brand new two-story cement and wood structures, within walking distance of the market. The very first day a

crowd of over twenty children stood in our doorway
craning their necks to get a look at the "long noses" who
had just moved to town. Paula stopped unpacking long
enough to give a short testimony and share with them
why we had come to Lamnarai.

In Bangkok, homes were enclosed by high walls and
we rarely interacted with busy neighbors caught up in
the urban rat-race. Here the rural Thai were more "laid
back" and always had time for friendly conversations.
The Bangkokians were used to foreigners; here we were
a curiosity.

It was easy for Paula and Ruthi to spend most of the
morning in the market, going from shop to shop buying
a few items and making small talk.   The market in this
frontier town was always a beehive of activity. Rickshaws,
tractors, carts, and motorcycles weaved in and out between shoppers. The only time they stopped was at eight
am and six pm, when the national anthem was played
over loudspeakers. As soon as the last note was played
the traffic would continue at its previous mad pace.

The sidewalks were almost as hazardous, with vendors
jostling one another for a choice spot as they solicited
customers. In Bangkok people were very fashion conscious, but here the latest trends were irrelevant. Men
wore long pants, thongs, and a button-up shirt tied at
the waist with a versatile *phakama*. This checkered strip
of cotton cloth is used as a turban, loincloth, towel and
even a hammock. The women wore colorful sarongs
with simple blouses which usually didn't match.

The daily trek to the market was quite a learning
experience. Paula and Ruthi had to learn the different
ingredients that make up Thai dishes, and bargain for
them at the proper price. In Bangkok, all our cooking
was done for us and was primarily foreign dishes along
with watered-down curry. Upcountry, cooking was a

different story. Foreign food was not appreciated by the Thai — they found it unfilling and bland. Paula once made her best fudge brownies for our neighbors, who wouldn't touch them. When another neighbor came to teach Paula a new dish, she said, "If you don't mind, I'd rather not use your gas stove. Do you have a hibachi?"

Paula learned to use spices like garlic, coriander and basil. She learned that a balanced meal had something spicy, bland, sweet and sour. The Thai can use around a dozen chilies in their spicy dishes, any one of which can blast the average foreigner out of his chair. We learned to avoid a pretty little orange chili called *prik kee nu luang* (which translated literally means, "yellow rat dropping"). Chopsticks weren't required; food is pushed onto the spoon with an overturned fork. On country visitation we learned to eat with our hands or with a single aluminum spoon from an enamel dish.

There are two rules for country dining: don't ask where the food came from or what it is made of. In the States I had said grace more out of habit than conviction. Here saying grace was in dead earnest, "May this food nourish our bodies ... (and not make us sick) ... Amen." When some rather fastidious relatives planned to visit, Paula began to panic. What could she serve them? My solution — tell them to bring frozen TV dinners on the plane!

Fortunately, the Lord provided a housegirl, Dewey, who was an adequate cook and taught Paula numerous dishes. Paula in turn taught Dewey about Jesus. She had a very rough home life and was bothered by evil spirits. Once Dewey came to our house scared, shaken and in no shape to work. She had been swimming in a pond when it seemed a hand grabbed her legs and tried to pull her under. When this happened a second time we explained to her from Ephesians chapter six about the spiritual battle, and prayed with her. After a few months Dewey made a profession of faith and was added to the emerging body of Christians in Lamnarai.

ELEVEN

DROPPINGS OF THE ANGELS

Go and report to John what you hear and see:
the blind receive sight and the lame walk, the lepers are cleansed
and the deaf hear, and the dead are raised up, and
the poor have the gospel preached to them.
(Matthew 11:4,5)

The most moving scene I witnessed in central Thailand was at a communion service. An elderly man carefully pressed a small plastic cup filled with grape soda between the two stumps he used for hands, and in the Thai fashion reverently bowed his head in gratitude for the shed blood of Jesus Christ, his Savior. As a young man he had used ten nimble fingers to plant tender rice seedlings in a flooded paddy. But as the years went by, he gradually lost the fingers on both hands, a victim of Thailand's most dreaded disease — leprosy.

My only previous exposure to leprosy had been through the Bible. In my mind a "leper" was a person with raw wounds in his flesh, a torn garment, and disheveled hair covering his mouth as he ran from others yelling, "Unclean, unclean, unclean ..." I was under the impression that leprosy was a highly contagious, loathsome, and incurable disease which infected not only people but garments and houses as well.

A Norwegian, G Armauer Hansen, discovered the

microbe causing leprosy in 1873. Hansen's disease, as it is now called, has ten million sufferers worldwide. Six million of those live in Asia and 400,000 in Thailand. Modern leprosy is not highly contagious and does not affect inanimate objects. In fact only 7% of those in close contact with the leprosy germ ever get it. At first I thought leprosy was like an acid which eats away a person's fingers and toes. Leprosy is actually a disease of the nervous system which causes the sufferer to lose feeling in his extremities. This means cuts and burns often go untreated, promoting infection and eventual loss of limbs.

In biblical times there was no treatment, but now powerful medicines can arrest the disease and make it non-communicable. All the leprosy sufferers I knew took pills to keep the disease in remission.

A common Thai expression for leprosy is *Rook Khi Thut* — the disease of angel's droppings. Buddhism teaches that "lepers" are suffering due to bad *karma,* some evil they committed in a previous existence. For the average male, the chief ticket to a better life in the next reincarnation is the monkhood, but this is barred to leprosy sufferers. As outcasts, they are sometimes denied service at the post office or a ticket on the bus.

This hostility is as bad as any racial prejudice and creates the same problems that AIDS does in the west. In developed areas leprosy is becoming more accepted, but in rural areas the fear and prejudice remain.

Once a distraught mother rushed her teenage daughter into our market house, pointing to a discolored white patch on the girl's ear. We told her she would have to wait for next week's clinic. She said she couldn't wait, and left in a panic to seek treatment. Since half of the church in central Thailand was affected by the disease, one of our main tasks was helping "well" believers understand the true nature of the disease and clearing up misconceptions.

A Christian Thai girl, Chiang, had the typical aversion to contacting people with leprosy. She was asked to give us language checks at Manorom Hospital, and we brought along a leprosy sufferer, Jinda, from Lamnarai to babysit while we studied. Jinda tried to get close to Chiang, but for Chiang it was a difficult adjustment. I often wondered how she felt when Jinda hugged her as young girls tend to do in Thai culture.

Chiang's biggest test came when Buzz invited her to a Bible study in the leprosy ward on the third floor of the hospital. A man named Riab opened the session with a new song he had just composed. One of Riab's eyes was distorted and looked off at an angle. When he leaned over too far his glasses would fall off what was left of his nose. One arm and a leg had been amputated. Despite Riab's appearance Chiang was impressed. Not only did he have a deep love for the Lord, he had also composed 45 songs for the Thai hymnal.

The patients were as curious about Chiang as she was about them, and asked her to share a testimony. During the Bible study a patient asked, "Chiang, we can understand God accepting people like ourselves, but why would you — *a well person* — want to believe in Jesus?"

By the end of the week Chiang's aversion to leprosy had subsided. One of my most treasured slides is of Chiang and Jinda sitting side by side in a swing with the smile of Christian fellowship on their lips.

Although not pretty on the outside, the leprosy sufferers of central Thailand have an inner strength and stickability not seen in the normal population. Why is there less "leakage" among leprosy converts? One author explains, "With the ordinary person, family pressures to keep up the habit of merit making at the temples are tremendous. To become a Christian is to become a social

outcast. But as leprosy sufferers are already outcast, they
tend to stand better. Unlike other Thai, they have everything to gain and little to lose by becoming Christians."[1] It is true they are not sensitive physiologically.
Burns and cuts often go unheeded and untreated.
Emotionally and spiritually, however, they are more
sensitive than the majority of what we call "well" people.

Over fifty percent of the Christians in central Thailand had their first contact with the gospel through
medical work. When I arrived in Lamnarai, the OMF
had 25 leprosy/skin clinics with 1,400 patients, run by
four nurses and six Thai paramedics. Once a month
either Buzz or I would collect tracts and a gospel poster
and drive the 15 kilometers to Chaibadan where the
clinic was held under the galvanized tin roof of an open
pavilion called a *sala*. On one side a queue of patients
waited to get their number or medicine. On the other,
two or three soaked their injured feet in aluminum pans
filled with a purple permanganate solution. The rest sat
and chatted on crude benches under the blistering heat
of the tin roof.

The atmosphere was ideal for evangelism. During the
six-hour clinic we had total freedom to share Christ.
When the nurses took a break we would pass out
hymnals, sing a few songs, and finish by preaching with
the aid of a poster. Some of the regulars even began to
memorize the hymns. The nurses always stuck a tract
among the leprosy control tablets, vitamins and anti-
anemia pills they distributed.

Feet are the least honored part of a Thai's anatomy.
The thought of touching even a well person's foot is
offensive to the Thai. At the *sala* I saw nurses not only
touch but gently cradle ulcerous limbs as they washed

[1]Leslie Lyall, *Urgent Harvest* (OMF Books), page 157

and bandaged them. Edith Barrett worked in north-east Thailand with the Christian and Missionary Alliance. Although not trained as a nurse, her job was to wash the feet of leprosy patients at their clinics. She lined her patients up in a row, starting with the less severe and ending with the more drastic cases. She told me, "Sometimes I would pray, 'come quickly, Lord Jesus, come quickly before I have to wash this last patient!'"

Monks in their saffron robes are among those who come for skin treatments. One monk observed a nurse washing a patient's foot and said, "Why, they do more than even a mother or father would do! The bandages and medicine they use must cost a lot, but they aren't in it for the money. They must have great love to touch people with *Rook Khi Thut*."

The *sala* at Chaibadan stood on property owned by Mr Hit. His original nickname, "Mr Itch", was given by missionaries who noticed him constantly scratching his skin. Such skin irritation is a common side effect of leprosy. The Thai found it difficult to pronounce "Itch" so they changed it to "Hit".

Mr Hit was born in 1936 to a poor family in central Thailand. At thirteen years old, while he was still a student, a strange discolored patch appeared on his ear. The headmaster was suspicious and took him personally to a doctor who diagnosed it as leprosy. When he returned to school he was no longer welcome — the first of many such rejections. Five years later the disease became debilitating, causing excruciating pain and sleepless nights. Ulcers appeared on Mr Hit's feet and his fingers began to gnarl and stiffen.

At the Lopburi clinic Hit heard the gospel for the first time. Emerson Frey held up a poster with a cross on it and spoke of how Jesus died on that cross for his sins. Hit thought, *If this isn't true, then why does this farang go to all this trouble to tell us about it? On the other hand, if it is true it must be worth studying. I'd like to know more.*

At 25 years of age, Hit and his family moved to an undeveloped tract of land outside of Chaibadan. There his leprosy deteriorated further. Someone told him that to get well he would need to see the *farang* doctors at a place called Manorom.

Manorom Hospital was started in 1956 and by 1959 had fifty beds. By 1960, 200 of the 300 converts in the region were influenced directly or indirectly by leprosy work centered at Manorom.

Hit borrowed $5 from his mother and left for the hospital. When he got to Lopburi he mispronounced the name and got lost, returning home depressed and disappointed. The hope of a cure, however, drove him to borrow another $5, and this time he made it safely.

At the hospital Hit was exposed to Bible studies in the leprosy wing, hymn singing with traditional Thai instruments and serious one-on-one discussions with the staff. He made a profession of faith, but before being baptized a convert had to pass an exam covering the fundamentals of the faith. This he failed. It was a crushing blow, yet his interest never wavered. Reflecting on that incident, Mr Hit told me, "The funny thing about the exam was that many of those who passed with flying colors failed to go on for the Lord." Eventually he passed and was baptized in a lily pond in front of the hospital. He went to Bible school for a while, but found the studies too advanced for his limited education.

In 1976, in his fortieth year, Mr Hit married a girl who also had leprosy, Miss Gong. It was the first marriage in the newly constructed Lopburi church. Hit and Gong are well suited to one another, and not just by way of temperament. When I introduced them to new missionaries I would say, "Just remember 'Hit the Gong' and you will have no problem!"

Before getting married Mr Hit was discipled by Ian Roberts, then stationed in Lopburi city. They struck up an immediate friendship, traveling thousands of miles by motorcycle sharing the gospel. They often spent the night in each other's homes. Ian tried to train Hit in Bible study and preaching. He found Bible reading and analysis difficult, but he knew how to meditate and draw appropriate applications from a passage. He will never be a preacher; his delivery is too emotionless and monotonous. Yet he is good in small groups, has the heart of an evangelist, and has led many family members to Christ. In seminary I studied four years of theology, much of it theoretical. Mr Hit was obviously no theologian, yet this unassuming man taught me more about practical Christian living than many hours in the classroom.

Hit is not much to look at. He is only 5 foot 3 inches tall and his skin is weathered by the tropical sun and wrinkled by leprosy. His glasses are always askew on what's left of his nose. The leprosy bacilli concentrate in the nose and cause the cartilage to collapse. Well-worn shoes protect his cracked and ulcerated feet. His hands are gnarled and twisted, but they can still wield a hammer with skill and precision.

Mr Hit is fairly well off; he owns his land debt free and with Gong's help has even saved for the future. Yet his shirts can be counted on one hand; he owns a $5 watch he cannot set, has no transportation, electricity, indoor plumbing or modern conveniences. Yet Mr Hit is content, more so than many Americans who have all the conveniences of the affluent west at their disposal. His contentment is not rooted in things or circumstances but in his personal relationship with Jesus Christ.

When I went out on evangelistic trips with Hit he

would often be called "Mr Disease," "Angel's droppings," or "Foreigner's slave". Even with persecution, bad health, and difficult circumstances, I never once heard him retaliate or complain.

On furlough I was amazed at the murmuring of secular society over the economy, politics, and even the weather. The same attitude seemed to spill over into the church, where members complained about everything from the pastor's sermons to the color of the rug in the foyer. Now when I am tempted to murmur, the memory of Mr Hit is enough to turn my grumblings into gratitude.

Working with leprosy sufferers like Mr Hit was rewarding on a personal basis, but often depressing when it came to church growth. It was difficult to convince "well" people to come to Christian meetings where leprosy patients are present. Twice we sent people interested in the gospel to the annual church camp near Manorom. As they watched the leprosy patients eating their meals, some binding utensils to the stump of their arm with rubber bands, they were turned off. Both lasted only a day and returned. When we asked them about it they said, *"Ahan mai long* — the food just wouldn't go down."

In Lamnarai "well" visitors were a rarity. It was easy to get disheartened over the lowly clientele of our church and the lack of success among the town's influential people. Then I came across a verse which totally changed my thinking — Luke 10:21, "I praise you, Father, Lord of heaven and earth, because you have hidden these things from the wise and learned, and revealed them to little children. Yes, Father, for this was your good pleasure." Was Jesus depressed when he looked at the ragtag group of disciples who followed him? No! Instead he thanked the Father for the wisdom of His electing grace. In the past I had acted as if God didn't know what He was doing with the Thai. Now I praise God that in His infinite wisdom He is using the "foolish, weak and base things" to confound the "wise and intelligent."

The sight of an elderly leprosy patient holding a communion cup was a moving enough scene, but what made it special was the verse I heard the pastor quote as he drank from the cup, "I will not drink of this fruit of the vine from now on until that day when I drink it anew with you in my Father's kingdom."

I thought about how one day this man would hold a communion cup with new hands and ten perfect fingers. He would no longer hobble but run; his indented nose would be reshaped and his cracking and leathery skin restored. No longer would he be ostracized, ridiculed and put down.

The Bible doesn't use the word "healed" when referring to people with leprosy; instead it uses the word "cleansed". This is fitting, because this elderly man will never be outwardly healed of the ravages of leprosy. He has, however, been cleansed inwardly and anticipates with joy the outer cleansing to come.

To this day when I hold a communion cup, I often think of that elderly man and say a prayer of gratitude to God for calling me to work among the leprosy sufferers of central Thailand.

TWELVE

THE FIRST SIX MONTHS

*I am convinced ... that Satan attempts more in that first year
or so of acclimati~ation in a foreign country than ever after.
(Doug Abrahams, OMF missionary to Japan)*

*It is the love of Christ that constrains us.
There is no other motivation for missionary service
that is going to survive the blows of even the first year.
(Elizabeth Elliot)*

At 2:30 am I was jarred out of a sound sleep by someone
searching through the headboard of the bed. Paula and
I sat up with a jerk; a thief was in our bedroom! My initial response was to send an ejaculatory telegram to God
as I screamed out in Thai, *"Chuay Duay!* Help, save me!"
The thief, clearly flustered, waved a knife and hissed at
us to be quiet. As my cries got louder and more persistant he decided to flee. He had used a chisel to remove
half of our front door!

I can't say we hadn't been warned. Just three months
earlier, veteran missionary David Robinson had predicted
that our first six months upcountry as church planters
would be the most difficult of our term if not our missionary career. His predictions were all too true. In that
brief span we would be robbed five times and spend
almost a month at hospital.

Petty theft is rife in Thailand.   There is not much armed robbery, but a great deal of robbery by stealth, break-ins, pickpockets, etc. One of the first lectures I heard at language school, given by the Thai headmaster, was on how to protect yourself from robbers. "Robber" (kamoy) was one of the first words I learned. When I brought a portable cassette player to class, a teacher told me how foolish I was to walk the streets with it. From then on I wrapped it in newspaper as a precaution. The headmaster warned women to protect their purses and men their pockets, especially in buses. Razor artists work the buses in teams and are experts at slitting purses, pockets and wallets.

In Bangkok you were always on the alert for motorcycle bandits. Once I was eating breakfast at Study House when a woman missionary was brought in crying and in obvious shock. On the way to breakfast, a kamoy had jumped off a motorcycle and tried to grab her gold necklace. When she resisted, he forced her to the ground and tore her blouse. Fear kept her from crying out, and although there were witnesses the thief escaped.

Upcountry had its share of motorcycle bandits too. I was warned not to ride my cycle at night in rural areas because robbers had been known to stretch a cable across the road in order to separate the hapless rider from his bike. In one lawless area, a missionary was stopped by robbers who not only took his motorbike but his clothes as well, forcing the poor man to walk back to town in his underwear!

Another notorious area was around Manorom Hospital. Manorom was said to be famous for four things: sweet pomelos (grapefruit), pretty girls, good rice, and robbers. People were often relieved of their motorbike at knife or gunpoint, but it was rare to hear of violence. Rowland Bell found it otherwise. One day in September

1976, he was traveling through some rice fields when he was attacked by thugs who hit him in the face with a log and stole his bike. For weeks his jellied face had to be supported by an intricate scaffolding.

I do not want to give the impression that Thailand is the only country with petty theft. Missionaries the world over must deal with thievery. In China, one couple found their housegirl selling clothes in the market — their clothes! A missionary in India had his glasses stolen in a crowded bus. The next day he saw a woman wearing them, and had to take them back by force. Koos Fietje had the same thing happen with a T-shirt he had hung out to dry. The young man who stole it didn't realize it had KOOS written in big letter across the front. Koos met the young man on the sidewalk one day and instructed him to return the shirt — immediately!

Lamnarai no doubt had its share of thieves and the possibility of being robbed had crossed our minds. What surprised us was the speed and intensity of the thieves there.

The first robbery occurred when we had been in Lamnarai just one week and had barely unpacked. I awoke after midnight and in my dazed state saw the screen door close behind a shadowy figure. My initial thought was that a demon was trying to frighten us. Yet as my eyes began to focus I saw that my jeans had vanished, along with over $200 for furniture in the pocket. In the morning I learned that the Curtis family had "entertained" the same visitor, with similiar results.

That morning we were expected at a conference near Manorom. Because of the robbery we missed our connections, and the trip took almost seven hours! The conference was only overnight, so by the time we arrived much of it was over. What made it worse was that when Ruthi took off Nathan's shoes, she found a dead, smelly frog inside. Yuk! In the confusion of the morning, she had shoved on his shoes, mortally wounding the inhabitant. Two-year-old Nathan never complained — maybe he liked it!

On our return three out of four adults plus the Curtis's son, Nathan, came down with fevers. Added to this the city water stopped flowing, Buzz was bitten by a dog, and Ruthi was hit by a tractor in the market. Then thieves struck again! This time they entered the kitchen, stealing knives and canned goods and leaving five banana peels on the floor.

Due to my illness, the task of reporting this incident to the police fell to Paula. The prospect of explaining the robbery to the authorities in Thai, however, was more than she could bear. In the end the robbery went unreported — an oversight we would later regret.

Both our families sensed the heat of spiritual battle increasing and wrote home seeking prayer ammunition to counteract Satan's darts. Ruthi wrote one prayer supporter, "What do you think the Lord is trying to teach us? I surely feel this is a terrible spiritual battle. God wants to do something in this town, that is why Satan doesn't want us around."

After I had run a fever for one week and Paula developed a sinus infection, our senior workers loaded us in their pick-up for the trip to Manorom. While waiting in emergency I overheard a doctor comment, "It's so sad what befalls our new missionaries." The doctor diagnosed my problem as glandular fever and prescribed three weeks of bed rest. I must have been quite a sight: Paula described me as a lethargic lump of clay.

When we returned to Lamnarai the first thing to do was to secure the houses. Ruthi described their fortifications, "Front door: two outside padlocks, two inside bolts and a padlock. Kitchen: sliding bolt and padlock. Back door and veranda: two sliding bolts and padlock. Bed-room: outside padlock and two inner bolts. Windows: bars and shutters." We also obtained a fierce dog and hired a watchman, and the police put us under special surveillance. I wrote confidently home, "Now our home is quite secure." Paula agreed, "Our home is burglar proof now — we hope."

For a couple of weeks life went normally. Then Andy came down with a fever. The local hospital couldn't help so six-month-pregnant Paula made the long journey to Manorom, changing buses three times. The last straw was after the third bus. They were at Chainat, only eight miles from the hospital, and it was turning dark. Paula asked if there was a taxi. Someone motioned to a drunk at a nearby table. He was the only driver around! Paula later described her feelings, "'Oh mercy, Jesus,' I hollered out. The usual fare was 75 cents but due to my desperate straits he asked $4. I said, 'OK, let's go'... well if you don't think I was praying ..." Despite the circumstances Andy began to feel cooler and by 7:30 pm the doctor pronounced him A-OK. Paula was not a little embarrassed.

Soon after this, we got word of the martyrdom of Koos Fietje. At the time we were consumed with our own problems and full of self-pity. Attending Koos' funeral helped put our "momentary light afflictions" in perspective.

A few days after the funeral, a conference was scheduled for all OMFers in central Thailand. It was the very night before we were to leave for the conference that Paula and I heard that ominous rumbling in our headboard. We had been instructed not to try and hinder a thief, yet I couldn't keep quiet. When the thief finally bolted for the door, I chased after him. By this time Buzz had been roused from sleep and joined me in the front yard. Inside, Paula was frantically searching for two-year-old Andy, sleeping under a mosquito net in another room. At first she couldn't locate him and thought he was kidnapped. She finally located him scrunched up in the corner of the net. With a sigh of relief she scooped him up and ran to the veranda where she fell to her knees in thanksgiving. Down below, Buzz and I were praying against Satan and singing songs. It must have been a queer sight.

People's reactions to such situations are highly unpredictable. A single worker in a neighboring town was going through her accounts when a man entered the house and pulled a gun, demanding money. On a reflex, she grabbed the man's hand and pointed the gun at the floor. The already nervous *kamoy* was so shocked that he ran out of the house without taking even one baht.

My favorite *"kamoy* story" comes from experiences in the life of Jane Addams, a nineteenth century social worker in Chicago. The first time a burglar entered her room she was more concerned for a sleeping nephew in the next room than herself. "Don't make a noise," she told the burglar. Startled, he leaped for a window. "You'll be hurt if you go that way," she said. "Go down by the stairs and let yourself out." The second time it happened Jane struck up a conversation with the thief. She learned he was just starting his career as a second-story man and didn't much care for it. She told him to come back the next day and she'd find him a job, which she did.

Unlike Jane's thief, ours didn't need any instructions. The gaping hole in our front door proved to me that he was quite familiar with the exits. My immediate problem was finding a way to plug it. Buzz helped locate some rough planks which we used to board up the hole, finishing just before daybreak.

At the conference there was a spontaneous outpouring of concern for the trials we were facing. A special time was set aside to pray for our families. Yet even as we prayed, thieves were entering the house of our superintendent in Nakorn Sawan and our house in Lamnarai — for the fourth time!

This time they got in by tearing off part of our kitchen wall, kicking in one door and breaking the locks off another. They took around $800 of merchandise including my cherished guitar and Paula's sewing machine. My mother wrote Paula, "I don't think you should feel too bad about the guitar ... after all, Larry never could sing too well." They took Paula's jewellery but for some reason passed over my gold wedding band.

As I surveyed our ransacked house my anger began to boil. I was angry at the *kamoys* who had humiliated my family and violated my home for two months. I was also angry at God for allowing it in the first place. It was then that God directed me to two convicting passages. Through Matthew 6:19ff, He seemed to be saying, "Larry, hold your earthly goods with a loose hand but cling to the true treasures in heaven where rust does not destroy nor *thieves* break in and steal." The second was Jonah 3:9-11, "And God said to Jonah (Larry), 'Is it right for you to be angry because of the plant that died (robbery)? ... You feel sorry for yourself when your shelter (house) is destroyed. And why shouldn't you feel sorry for a great city like Ninevah with its 120,000 people (Lamnarai had 10,000) in utter spiritual darkness." These verses showed me I was getting more upset over the robberies than over the dying souls all around me.

Although the anger subsided, we were still jittery. The first night we returned from the conference, Paula refused to even sleep in the house. For the next couple of weeks our sleep was fitful at best. Every sound sent us downstairs to check.

Paula became unusually leery of the Thai. When she reached for her purse to pay for groceries one day, the purse was gone. Frantically she looked around. A suspicious-looking man was standing at the counter. Just as she was ready to cry, "Help ... *kamoy!*" she felt something under her arm — the purse had been there all the time!

The Thai were jittery too and it became difficult to find watchmen. Those who agreed to come brought weapons, others suggested we move to another part of town. Some tried to reassure us, "Don't worry, Thai robbers are after things not people," yet sleep continued to elude us. During this period, Paula came across Proverbs 19:23 and fashioned a plaque with the words, "The fear of the Lord leads to life, so that one may sleep satisfied, untouched by evil." 2 Timothy 1:7 was also comforting, "For God has not given us a *spirit of fear* but of power and love and of a sound mind."

After installing a metal door, new locks, more surveillance and a fierce dog, both Paula and I began to rest easier. Yet when we returned from Bangkok on December 2 we had been robbed again — number five!

On December 4, a full three months after the first break in, the police finally had a suspect for us to identify. They told us, "Don't be afraid," but that didn't keep our hearts from racing. The man they showed us was not the one who had entered our bedroom, and so we returned home disappointed. A few minutes later, the police had another suspect. This time Paula paused and prayed for wisdom. The future of a young man hung in the balance and she wanted to be a hundred percent sure. God made the identification easy — the suspect was wearing one of Paula's necklaces! The police took me into an inner room. "Is this yours?" he asked, as he held up the splintered remains of my cherished Gerard tenor guitar.

Outside Paula met the young man's distraught mother, who asked, "How do you know for sure it was my son who robbed you?"

Paula replied, "I saw him in my bedroom with a knife, and he was wearing my necklace just now."

The mother shook her head, "Well, that figures — he has always been a bad boy, constantly in trouble." A church member joined in at this point and shared God's forgiveness, assuring her that we were not angry or desiring vengeance.

What followed was a month of litigation, hours at the police station and reams of reports. The police even brought the suspect into our bedroom to reenact the crime! Whenever he contradicted my testimony, the investigating officer slapped his head with a clipboard. I tried to tell him that I didn't desire vengeance, only justice, but he didn't seem to listen.

I knew the root problem of the two suspects was spiritual, and sought a way to speak with them. After their arrest I went to the jail with food and some tracts in a bag. But when I explained my intentions to the jailer, he turned me away. "Aren't these the men who robbed you? Don't feel sorry for them. They are just animals."

Since the case was proceeding slowly, Paula and I decided to take a trip to Manorom. While we were there, a policeman tracked me down and ordered me back to Lamnarai. After four hours on the road I arrived at the Lamnarai police station, asking, "What's so urgent?"

The officer said, "I need you to sign your name to your testimony." Eight hours round trip with six connections just to sign my name?

The document they wanted me to sign was in Thai legal language. "How do I know what I am signing?" I asked. For all I knew, it could have been a confession that I had done the crime myself.

"Don't worry," the officer assured me, "we've taken care of everything."

Soon afterwards the two suspects were sentenced to prison, and Paula and I breathed a sigh of relief.

In those four months I learned more about prayer than in the previous four years. We found that God may seem slow in answering prayer but He is never late; a delay is not necessarily a denial.

From the beginning, fellow workers, churches and individuals were interceding on our behalf. Their perseverance was rewarded. Luke 18 makes it clear that God is not an unprincipled judge who must be worn down to administer justice. In our case justice was not denied, merely delayed. Ben Franklin once said, "Those things that hurt instruct." God used what we felt was a hurtful delay to instruct us spiritually and build godly qualities in our lives.

We came to appreciate the OMF family in a new way. A single missionary with limited funds gave us a generous check to buy a new sewing machine. When we were sick OMFers babysat Andy, watched our house, nursed our fevers and drove us to the hospital. The love and concern which had drawn me to the mission in the first place was continued in Thailand.

The primary lesson we learned was concerning Satan's character and strategy. During the Normandy invasion of World War II, the Allies' primary task was to establish a beachhead from which they could launch an all-out attack. The hardest fighting came during those initial assaults. Our "Normandy" was Lamnarai, and the enemy was using robberies and sickness to destroy our beachhead.

Paul must have felt the same way in Corinth, as recorded in Acts 18, when Satan was harrassing and attacking him. How wonderful of the Lord to draw near in a vision and say, "Do not be afraid, keep on speaking, do not be silent. For I am with you, and no one is going to attack you in order to harm you, for I have many people in this city." God had plans for Lamnarai as well, plans which could not be frustrated or aborted by the schemes of Satan.

THIRTEEN

CULTURE SHOCK

It is not good for the Christian's health
To hustle the Asian brown;
For the Christian riles,
And the Asian smiles
And he weareth the Christian down.
And the end of the fight
Is a tombstone white
With the name of the late deceased
And an epitaph drear:
"A fool lies here
Who tried to hustle the East."
(Rudyard Kipling)

Having worked as a journalist in India for seven years, Kipling had experienced the stress of adjusting to a new culture. In this poem he may be describing a new missionary he observed being "worn down" physically and emotionally in his effort to convert nationals. What Kipling described in poetic form is a phenomenon which today we call culture shock.

Culture shock is impossible to describe: you must experience it. It reminds me of my first encounter with manual transmission. It looked easy, but there was a great deal of gear grinding and neck jerking before the gears meshed smoothly together. Shifting gears from

West to East had a similiar effect. When my occidental lifestyle encountered the oriental lifestyle ... sparks began to fly.

At first the term "culture shock" evoked an image of physical trauma in my mind. Is it like jumping into a tank of ice water, or putting your finger in a light socket? No. It is a much more subtle and gradual process, yet just as dangerous.

As familiar cultural clues and props are slowly removed, you find yourself becoming increasingly irritable, fatigued and resentful. A simple act like going to the store, writing a check or sending a letter can produce grave anxiety. The realization that you are an alien in a foreign land begins to sink in, causing disillusionment and a feeling of helplessness. Doctors of missiology call it "cultural disorientation", but don't let them fool you — culture shock is nothing more than acute homesickness.

As a new worker I identified with John-Mark in Acts 13. Some commentators maintain that the reason Mark abandoned Paul and Barnabas at Perga was fear of persecution or disease in Asia Minor. I have a simpler theory; Mark was just plain homesick. Like many new workers in similiar circumstances, Mark longed for his friends, mother's cooking and the creature comforts of home.

I remember being homesick my first day of school and during two weeks of church camp. In both cases I recovered because I knew I would soon be home. Acute homesickness is different. It is the feeling I had when I realized that six months of our term had passed, but that still left 42 before furlough. I knew I had the disease when I started passing up Christmas presents in order to read the local newspapers used as packing material! Paula tried to relieve her homesickness by writing letters home. The volume of mail to her parents was under-standable, but 125 letters to a mother-in-law?

Besides homesickness we also experienced what is known as "role shock". One of the most humbling aspects of mission work is changing from the role of leader to follower. I arrived in Thailand with a Masters degree and experience in business and ministry. Yet my under-standing of Thai culture and language was that of a kindergarten student. Accomplishments or degrees from the west meant nothing. I felt like an idiot. I couldn't read a simple label or even ask where the bus let off passengers. What made it worse was the fact that our son was adjusting well and picking up quickly on the language. The time would come when we would be able to teach and lead, but for now our role was to learn and follow.

Trying to sort out your role as a foreigner isn't easy. Paula thought she would "go native" and wear the traditional *sarong* in order to identify with the Thai. By doing so she would be following in the steps of OMF's founder, Hudson Taylor, who adopted Chinese dress in order to identify with the Chinese. It sounded like a good plan. One Sunday she wore her most colorful *sarong* to church.

At the service a woman asked, "Why did you wear that?"

"I thought I was supposed to," Paula replied inno-cently.

"Don't you know you are an *ajarn* (respected tea-cher)?" the woman retorted. "*Ajarns* don't wear *sarongs!*" Paula never wore a *sarong* to church again.

In Thailand it is easy to make such cultural blunders. A Thai walks slowly and softly, doesn't point with his feet or touch anyone's head. So if you are used to stomping about, using your foot as a third hand or ruffling people's hair, you are in for trouble.

The Mormons learned this lesson the hard way. The blunder which two young Mormon missionaries made in Thailand is still used in their orientation course as the classic example of *what not to do*. The two missionaries took each other's pictures sitting on the head of a Buddhist statue. They sent the film to Bangkok for processing, and the photo-shop forwarded the picture to a local newspaper who published it, causing public outrage. Within a short time all Mormon missionaries were instructed to leave the country.

These two naive Mormons learned a lesson in Thai anatomy the hard way. Every Thai knows that the head is the highest and most revered part of the body, and the feet are the lowest. Sitting with your feet dangling over the face of a statue (the Buddha no less) is cultural suicide.

Today most new missionaries have extensive training in Thai culture and traditions — older missionaries weren't as fortunate. Margot Simpson, a nurse from Scotland who had been in Thailand over twenty years, told us, "I'm just beginning to understand what acclimatization and acculturation is all about. In those days we were going through culture shock but didn't know what to call it. Back then there was no orientation or introductory classes to Thai culture. In those days we just jumped straight into the work."

On the surface Thai society is modest and reserved, especially concerning dress and showing affection in public. Separation of the sexes is the norm, and in many up-country churches the men sit on one side and the women on the other. We were told it was inappropriate even for married couples to hug, kiss, or hold hands in public. Breaking this code can lead to serious consequences. The brother of one of our church members playfully grabbed the waist of a single girl during a village festival. The parents of the girl took that action as a "proposal" and demanded a shot-gun wedding, even though there had been no sexual misconduct.

So imagine my shock when a male Bible college student grabbed my hand and started walking with me to a chapel service. Such an action has no homosexual overtones here, as in the west, but is a common sign of friendship among young people of the same sex. As a westerner I felt uncomfortable to say the least, but I now accept it as yet another Thai trait.

In the past there was no way for a missionary to measure how much stress he was under or how close to cultural "burnout" he might be. Now new missionaries can calculate how much pressure they are facing through the social readjustment rating scale devised by Dr Thomas Holmes — the Holmes stress chart.

Each point on the Holmes' scale is called a "life-change unit" or LCU. An accumulation of more than 200 LCUs in any one year could be potentially dangerous both physically and emotionally. Death of a spouse is highest at 100. Even happy events like Christmas or vacations are worth 10 LCUs. The birth of a baby rates 39. Many experts advise not to have a child anywhere near cross-cultural transition. This is good advice, but for us it wasn't practical — Paula was pregnant twice during our first term.

During our first six months in central Thailand we were robbed repeatedly, Paula delivered our second child, we moved house, studied a new language, changed jobs and the whole family was sent to the hospital for various illnesses. Myron Loss, who wrote a book on culture shock, estimated that the *normal* first termer is running at or above 400 LCUs. Ours being an *abnormal* first term must have pushed the LCUs past the 500 mark at times.

When you are functioning at this stress level, the chances of going into "shock" are high.

The Holmes chart is helpful in measuring major changes like illness, birth or death but it overlooks seemingly insignificant inconveniences which are equally debilitating. To correct this oversight I have devised the Dinkins social readjustment scale:

15 LCU	having to fish live mosquito larvae out of your cereal bowl
20 LCU	plugging a 110 volt appliance into a 220 volt outlet
8 LCU	having to tear all correspondence into small pieces (the locals make bags out of scrap paper)
18 LCU	a four-hour bus ride that stretches into eight
12 LCU	finding a fly floating in a new bottle of fish sauce
7 LCU	bargaining for everything from taxi rides to vegetables
10 LCU	not being able to point your feet, hold hands, wear shoes inside and other cultural "No-nos"
18 LCU	your chicken soup includes the head and feet as well
16 LCU	opening a gift of chocolate from home, only to find it melted and ant-infested.

Another category that should be added to the Holmes chart is:

22 LCU a military coup d'etat

Coming from the United States, I was used to a stable government with a 200-year-old constitution. Thailand, on the other hand, has endured fourteen military coups since 1947, along with numerous changes of the constitution. The Thai seem to take such political changes in stride and advise foreigners to keep a "cool heart". But when you see tanks in the public park and hear of people being shot it is hard to keep your cool. The American embassy assured us that there were "contingency plans" in the event of real trouble, but that was of little comfort. The two coups we witnessed did not force us to flee the country but they did remind us that our time in Thailand could be cut short and that we must "redeem the time" while it lasted.

The ultimate inconvenience was a "blackout" which our town had all too frequently. Sometimes in April when the temperature was over 100 degrees inside the house, you could hear a simultaneous "Oh no!" as the electric supply was cut off and the fans stopped turning. When that happened all you could do was sit, sweat, soak, pray and watch the fans for any sign of movement. When the fans started up again you would hear another yell in the neighborhood, "Hurray!"

We had just finished saying "Hurray!" one time when we realized it was a bit premature — now the water supply was shut off. We simply redirected our prayers from the electric department to the water department.

Housegirls are a notorious source of stress for new missionaries. The theory is that a housegirl will relieve pressure on the missionary wife by doing common chores and cooking food. But sometimes the opposite is true. Our first housegirl was nicknamed "fatty" but was in fact skinny as a rail. We ended up hiring, firing, and then rehiring her when no other help was available. During our second term we went through seven housegirls which is a record we plan to submit to the *Guinness Book of Missionary Records*. Paula once expressed the sentiments of many, "Can't live with them and can't live without them."

One tribal girl named Joni almost ended Paula's

missionary career. Paula asked her to light our gas stove
one day, but didn't realize that as a Hmong from the
mountains of north Thailand, Joni had never used a
modern stove, though she could do wonders on a char-
coal-burning brazier. After leaving the gas open for a few
minutes she returned the matches to Paula complaining
that the stove wouldn't work. Paula leaned over the
open door with year-old Titus in one hand and a lighted
match in the other ... BLAM! A blast of hot gas knocked
her back, singeing the hair on her arm. Mustering all
her strength, she tried to appear calm and said softly,
"Joni ... next time try to light the match *first,* then turn
on the gas, DO YOU UNDERSTAND?!"

Tourists who pass through Thailand are whisked from
airport to luxury hotel in airconditioned coaches, and
eat only the best of foods. To them, Thailand is romantic, picturesque and exotic. The tourists who have stayed
with us, however, get a different view of the "Land of
Smiles". A friend from seminary asked if he and his wife
could visit our up-country home and see missionary life
as it really is. Roc and his wife Bev were not disappointed.

After a long, hot taxi ride Bev was dying for a shower
so we directed her to the bathroom. There she was
faced with a dilemma. The bathroom in our house was
only 3 by 9 feet, with a hole in the floor for a toilet.
There was no shower; you bathed by scooping water
with a plastic bowl from a trough and then sluicing it
over your body. After a few minutes, Bev called despair-
ingly to Roc, "Honey, do you think you could help me in
here?" Paula and I couldn't help laughing as they dis-
cussed strategy, bathed, and then emerged together from
their confined space cleaner but a bit shaken.

My father was also a bit shaken the first time he
entered a Thai bathroom. We had written him often

concerning our problems with theft, so when he entered our bathroom he exclaimed, "Son, it looks like someone stole your toilet as well!"

When Paula's pastor from California visited, we could tell he was having a rough time with the heat and humidity. Once I caught him spreadeagled on the linoleum floor, trying to take a nap. I asked him, "Lenox, why don't you use the bed?"

"I've figured out that it's cooler down here," was his reply.

One of the best cultural shock absorbers we discovered was the simple phrase "It's not *wrong*, it's just *different.*" Our immediate gut reaction in many situations was, "Don't you know you are doing that all wrong?" Eventually, however, we realized that there is nothing ethically or morally wrong with bare feet indoors, driving on the left side or even holding hands with people of the same sex. It may be *different* but it's not *wrong*.

Obviously, the best shock absorbers are spiritual. During difficult times Paula was fond of quoting out loud, "For this I have Jesus ... For this I have Jesus ..." At times of stress it was also helpful to reconfirm God's call. We knew that God had specifically called us to Thailand, and to the situations and lifestyle that were a part of that call. There was no sense in fighting His will. We found that things went much better when we accepted His leading and sovereignty over the circumstances of our lives. Amy Carmichael expressed it well when she wrote, "In acceptance lieth peace."

Hudson Taylor once made a plaque for new workers undergoing the rush and bustle of life in China. It was a stanza from the great hymn "Be Still My Soul" by Katharina von Schlegel:

Be still my soul: the Lord is on thy side;
Bear patiently the cross of grief and pain;
Leave to thy God to order and provide;
In every change He faithful will remain.
Be still my soul, thy best, thy heavenly Friend
Through thorny ways leads to a joyful end.

There is still no better antidote to culture shock, or common stresses encountered in the west either, than the formula stated in this song. If the Christian in Kipling's poem could only have understood this principle, the epitaph on his grave would have read differently.

FOURTEEN

NO BIG NAMES

*Notice among yourselves dear brother, that few of you who
follow Christ have big names or power or wealth.*
(Paul — 1 Corinthians 1:26 TLB)

The core group that met each Sunday in Lamnarai was
not much to look at by the world's standards: a reformed
alcoholic, his illiterate wife, an orphan, a leprous merchant twice divorced, and a leprous carpenter with his
family. Not exactly the type of people you would choose
as the charter members of a new church! Yet God de-
lights to choose these kind of people to perform His
sovereign plan. I Corinthians 1:27 says, "God has chosen
the *foolish* things of the world to shame the wise, and
God has chosen the *weak* things of the world to shame
the things which are strong." God was slowly forming
this group of five or six believers, foolish and weak by
worldly standards, into a church which would someday
shame both the wise and the strong in Lamnarai.

One of those who had professed Christ before we
came to Lamnarai was Auntie Tam's husband, Chan. If
there ever was a Thai who deserved the title "character",
it was Uncle Chan. Andy mispronounced Chan as Chang
(elephant), so from then on he was always Uncle Elephant. His trademark was a tattered wide-brim grey hat
which he wore low on his wrinkled brow. His shoes were

tire retreads and he often wore a T-shirt advertising a farm product or brand of liquor. His wiry 5-foot 3-inch frame was surprisingly agile. I'll always remember the time this 60-year-old grandfather climbed a tamarind tree and hung by one arm like a monkey. His spindly weather-worn hands were usually rolling tobacco in newspaper or a dried banana leaf — smoking was one vice he never seemed able to conquer.

Gum disease had reduced Chan's smile to a virtually toothless grin. His speech would have challenged even a PhD in linguistics. He spoke rapidly in a slurred staccato which seemed to break all the rules of Thai pronunciation. Socrates learned oratory by speaking with his mouth full of pebbles — Uncle Chan sounded like he forgot to remove the pebbles. With Chan the "knowing nod" was particularly useful.

Chan made a living by selling herbal medicine, while Tam supplemented their income by marketing dried fish. A sack of herbal cures was Chan's constant companion, and sometimes he would sneak off by the roadside to replenish his stock. He believed, like many rural Thai, that the body consisted of four elements: water, fire, wind, and earth. Illness was simply an imbalance of these elements, a condition Chan claimed his remedies would restore.

I remember vividly his cure for a sore throat. A mother brought her sick daughter to Chan, who examined the girl and then mixed up a herbal ointment with mortar and pestle. Taking some of the paste on his forefinger, he tried to coat the child's throat. The little girl vomited immediately. Always quick on his feet, Chan responded calmly, "See how quickly it worked; the poison has come out of her body already!"

Chan advertised his potions as "God's medicine" and spread what he knew about Jesus as well as his medicine over a wide area. His theology wasn't that sound, and we constantly warned him not to attack his previous faith or say Jesus fulfilled an office similiar to a Buddhist Messiah.

Despite flawed theology and fluctuating temperament, Auntie Tam was still grateful for the changes she saw in her husband. Instead of searching for alcohol or women, he was searching his Bible daily. To Tam this was the greatest miracle of all. Before his conversion Chan was functionally illiterate, but now when he picked up a Bible or hymnal he could read with understanding.

The strongest member of the church was Mrs Saijai, who had moved her noodle shop from Lopburi City to Lamnarai. Saijai's maturity proved a real asset to the fledgling church. Meetings were held in her home, at first monthly, later weekly.

Mr Hit began to bring relatives to these meetings and some were converted. Even his 65-year-old mother came to Christ. Grandma Tan looked like she just stepped out of the nineteenth century. Like many elderly women, she wore her hair in a crew-cut, a custom started 200 years ago when the Burmese were threatening to invade Siam. The king ordered women to cut their hair short and dress like men to make the Burmese think they had a large number of troops.

Grandma Tan wore her sarong in the *jong-kraben* style, in which two ends of the sarong are brought together in front, stretched tight and then rolled tightly from top to bottom. The two ends are then pushed between the legs and brought up to the small of the back where it is held in place by a belt.

We called her our "betel nut granny" because she was always chewing this product of the areca palm and spitting a bright red stream of juice. Grandma would place the grated and dried betel along with red lime paste on a small leaf and then stuff the roll in her mouth. The betel stained her teeth and made her mouth bright red. The betel nut or *mahk* is such a staple that one Thai proverb for hard times says, "Rice is hard to get and *mahk* expensive." *Mahk* is as addictive as tobacco, and although Grandma Tan tried to quit she gave up the effort when her teeth began to hurt.

As much as I enjoyed working with the Lamnarai Christians, I still had a longing to teach. So when an opportunity came to teach a short course at a Bible School in North Thailand, I jumped at it. The Bible Training Center at Phayao was started in 1966 by OMF to train both Thai and tribal people in the Scriptures. The school sits on a bluff overlooking a placid lake framed by a green mountain range. The students help defray their tuition costs by raising pigs, cattle, crops, and harvesting rice. The guest house we stayed at was nice but it had no heating. Coming from the hot plains, we were unprepared for cool temperatures; and ended up sleeping in one bed with our clothes on to keep warm. A large snake had the same idea and took up residence under the bed. Four brave students helped exterminate the intruder.

I was to teach a Bible Study Methods course to 45 students in the first year class. Many of them had only a fourth grade education. I started each class by distributing a handout to each student. Somehow I miscounted and was always one short. One day the last handout was set on a desk before two male students. Both reached for it at once. When one grabbed the paper from the other a shoving match began which escalated into a full-fledged fist fight. My seminary professors had taught me nothing about refereeing boxing matches, so I was most grateful for a student who stepped in to quell the riot.

The two students turned pugilists were too big to

spank so I sent them to the principal. He explained to me that one of them had been a gang leader and the other a communist before coming to the school. Students with such backgrounds are not uncommon. Recently 15 out of 45 in the first year class trusted Christ for the first time.

I didn't envy the principal's job. Besides being an administrator and teacher, he acted as chaperon as well. Once he stayed up all night in a pick-up truck on a stakeout, trying to catch a couple who were breaking curfew.

The prayer card I had printed before leaving for the field said, "Larry Dinkins — Bible teaching in Bangkok, Thailand." The Area Director felt that this was a worthy goal, but it didn't fit with mission policy: new workers were sent upcountry to gain experience before further designation. My month at Phayao confirmed the wisdom of this.

Jesus told his disciples, "... everyone after he has been *fully trained,* will be like his teacher" (John 6:40). I was far from being "fully trained" and was nowhere near ready to be a professor. My role was that of student, not teacher. Right now I had a more urgent task — passing lab work in Lamnarai.

FIFTEEN

LAMNARAI LAB

OMF's goal: "... to plant a church in every community and thereby to bring the gospel to every creature."

Before coming to Lamnarai I had asked a senior worker, "What works here in Thailand?" As a westerner I was used to methods, tracts, and strategies which would statistically produce x number of conversions. Reading *Peace Child* by Don Richardson made me think that Thai culture too might contain a redemptive analogy which would unlock their hearts to the gospel. To my disappointment my friend replied, "Frankly, Larry, nothing works. You will have to experiment and find your own method." That is just what we did for the next three years in our lab in Lamnarai — experiment.

Even with limited language you can always try literature distribution. From the first day in the market we started to hand out tracts. In the course of three years we must have handed out thousands, but only got three responses back in the mail. Our sales from the book trolley weren't much better, but we could always attract a crowd by putting Andy or Nathan in the carriage under the trolley. Once a year we sold contest books in schools. This generated many sales and enrolled hundreds of children in correspondence courses. At Christmas we put on programs in these schools which drew large crowds, some as large as 1300 students.

Next to literature the method we relied on most was film and slide shows. Each dry season we loaded up a green Isuzu pickup with movie equipment to make a tour of nearby villages. The method of showing movies had not changed since the Gospel Rover days of the 1950's. You simply found a suitable spot, cranked up the generator, played music to attract a crowd, and erected a cloth screen. Putting up the screen was a bit unnerving — it was full of bullet holes. Next we announced the program for that night: Creation of the World, Flood, or "Jesus" based on the gospel of Luke. After seeing these stories around 25 times I could almost say the parts myself.

At dusk, vendors set up trolleys around the area and up to 500 villagers, some with flashlights, converged on the site like so many lightning bugs. Most people thought we were a traveling medicine show and asked what we were selling. They were surprised to hear it was free. When the movies ended, around midnight, the area emptied within five minutes. The next day would be spent trying to follow up those who had attended.

At other times we brought in a theatrical troupe to present the gospel in a traditional form called *likey*. The best performer was a woman, so she was selected to play the part of Jesus. In the climactic crucifixion scene this woman, dressed in a white sequined outfit, was lifted up on a cross. My western sensibilities found this hard to accept but the Buddhist Thais responded well to the presentation.

Cassette players proved to be a great help to the semiliterate Christians in Lamnarai. We had a library of 150 tapes which featured questions and answers, sermons, teaching and music.

However tapes were not meant to replace fellowship

and worship together.   Within a week or so of arriving in Lamnarai I was called upon to give the sermon at the Sunday meeting in Mrs Saijai's narrow shophouse. Five or six Thai sat cross-legged in a circle to hear the new missionary preach.   In seminary I was used to people critiquing my sermons, but never while I was delivering them! After every other sentence Saijai would interrupt to correct a faulty vowel or tone.

The "call of nature" caused further interruptions. Thai culture dictates that the head of a person entering or leaving a room must be lower than the heads of those present.   Since we were seated on the floor already, Granny Tan had to crawl out on her hands and knees with her nose almost touching the floor.   Between Mrs Saijai's analysis of my sermon and Granny Tan's exit, it was all I could do to finish the passage.

When attendance increased to ten the church moved to a school.   I was happy.   At least there would be no more crawling.   After we wore out our welcome at the school, a lean-to shelter was built on Uncle Chan's land, with a rough concrete floor and benches on three sides. It wasn't much to look at; but God's presence was felt there as much as in any cathedral.

I had been raised in a church with a massive pipe organ and trained choir. Here it was *a capella* all the way. It took a while for new converts to adjust to singing. At the Buddhist temple they were used to chanting but not singing. As songleader I tried to help them with new tunes, but since my gift is definitely not music the result was less than melodious. Sometimes I would start a song too high or too low and we would have to start over. Two words would describe our music ministry — a "joyful noise".

What the church members lacked in musical ability, they made up in volume — especially Uncle Chan. Uncle

Chan's favorite song was number 10, "The Heart of Man". He sang it with great gusto. This song describes in detail the depraved heart of man and Christ's power to cleanse it. I believe Chan chose it because it spoke clearly of his spiritual condition before trusting Christ. However, he never was able to find No. 10 in his hymnal. He had learned to read but had never mastered Thai numbers. So before each song we had to wait until Chan and a few others could find their place. In the west we say, "he sings like a crow" but in Thailand they say, "he sings like a water buffalo." Uncle Chan's voice fit that description perfectly.

Once a month Pastor Jarern from a town sixty miles away would come to help with song leading and preaching. Leprosy had caused Jarern to lose first his job as a teacher and then his wife. He later remarried a Christian and was discipled by OMF missionaries. Jarern was not as badly marred as others with leprosy. His feet and one hand were affected, but his broad face appeared normal. A booming voice and experience teaching school complemented a very evident spiritual gift of pastor-teacher.

Since Jarern visited us monthly we began to regard him as a spiritual mentor. We appreciated his cultural insights, ability as a counselor, and discernment in dealing with the Thai. As foreigners we were easily fooled by Thai who showed interest, hoping Christianity would be a means of material gain. We needed someone like Jarern to separate the "professors" from the "possessors".

After much follow-up and sharing, a man in our community professed Christ publicly in March. By November we heard he was in jail charged with robbery. Nominalism continues to be a problem among church members in Thailand. Jarern made a pastoral call on a member who had been missing services and asked, "Have you looked at your Bible today?" He replied, "Why yes, pastor, I looked at it just this morning — to make sure the rats hadn't eaten it."

Having the church on Chan's land increased opposition from neighbors and within his own family. Chan's stepson was a particular problem. Once he drew the name of Jesus on the sole of his shoe and then stomped it in the dirt: "If God is real why doesn't he break my neck right now — I dare Him." Uncle Chan told me he could take abuse as a father, but when his stepson blasphemed his Father in heaven, it was more than he could bear.

During this time I visited the home of a fellow worker. On the wall was the picture of a bug-eyed kitten hanging for dear life over a big abyss. I thought to myself, *Lord, that's how I feel. The antagonism and nominalism of this place is getting to be too much. Any moment I could lose my grip and fall into the abyss of discouragement.* It was then I noticed the caption "HANG IN THERE!"

One village which encouraged us to hang on was a small hamlet situated in the midst of a vast sea of rice — Green Island. In Lamnarai, we were used to electricity, running water, and toilet facilities. The poor leprosy Christians at Green Island had none of these conveniences, but they did have a desire to learn more about Christ. From our base in Lamnarai we visited this outpost almost every week for two years. At first we had a rather cold reception. People threw rocks at us, and one man tried to pick a fight with members of our team.

Gradually the village people became more receptive to our message. One day after we had given a poster talk, a young man stepped forward and boldly announced his desire to follow the God of the Christians. His name was Jiam.

Jiam was a poor, illiterate rice farmer with three children, who lived in a one-room bamboo shack. His sordid past and inability to read made follow-up difficult; but he loved to listen to the gospel and often played tapes on high volume so the neighbors could hear. Later he destroyed all the occult material in his house. His youngest daughter had her foot burned in a campfire, fusing the toes together and making walking difficult.[1] Buzz asked his supporters back home to pray for her and they responded by sending money to pay for an operation for the child at Manorom Hospital.

After we had visited Green Island regularly for two years, Jiam and seven others were ready to be baptized. On September 9, 1983, we drove two pickup-loads of believers to witness the ceremony. Pastor Jarern performed the baptism in a shallow pond surrounded by rice paddies, and Mr Hit dunked the candidates. Mr Hit became concerned when Auntie Boonmee failed to come up, and so pulled her up by her hair. Boonmee exclaimed, "Why did you do that? You didn't give me time to finish my prayer!" Apparently she wanted to pray underwater to more effectively "seal" her salvation.

At the conclusion of the ceremony, we returned to Green Island for a parade. Around forty believers marched behind a large banner of John 14:6, singing songs and handing out tracts. The day ended with the presentation of baptism certificates and flowers to each of the eight new Christians. That day was truly the highlight of our first term.

The next week I asked the congregation if they got a blessing from last week's *piti sop*. I meant to say *piti baptisma* (baptism ceremony), but the word *sop* which means "funeral" came out instead. When no one volun-

[1]This story is told in the children's book *NEW TOES FOR TIA*

teered I asked again, "Who got a blessing from the *funeral?*" After three times the congregation was feeling uneasy and didn't know how to respond. Finally, one member felt sorry for me and held up her hand. The members were already rolling in the aisles with laughter by the time I realized my error.

The baptisms at Green Island were encouraging, but after three years in Lamnarai we were still waiting for a breakthrough there. The five members had increased to nearly twenty, yet the leadership was far from strong and some members were at best "nominal".

Almost every new worker passes through periods of despair when he wonders if his presence in Thailand is really worth it. The stranglehold of Buddhism and idolatry seems too strong and the results meager. He receives reports from colleagues in other fields who are enjoying the fruits of revival while his own work languishes.

In such situations it is easy to listen to Satan's accusing voice: "Larry, do you really think these Thai are listening to you? As soon as you leave here they will be back in my clutches. Look at your church — a handful of illiterate lepers. How can they amount to anything? I've controlled this area for hundreds of years, what makes you think you can change things. Fat chance. And what about your friends back home? Do you honestly think they are praying for you? They don't care."

I expected such attacks from Satan but it came as a surprise to receive similiar accusations from well-meaning supporters back home. Once I received the following letter: "I have been reading your letters for years now and for some reason I haven't seen any progress in your endeavors. Maybe I am not reading them carefully enough. Have you established a local church yet? Have you discipled a young man to be the pastor of the church when you go on to another village? Am I mistaken in my understanding of what a missionary should do? Please explain your concept of missionary work."

God knew my gloomy state after reading this letter and so prompted another supporter to write the following note that same week, "Don't be discouraged. Our Lord measures success far differently than man does. If your efforts are predestined to bring even one to Christ for future work in His kingdom, and if you preach to a crowd of thousands and reach that one, in Christ's eyes you are a hundred percent successful. Don't be *misled or discouraged.*"

The situation in Thailand is similar to what Paul faced in the idolatrous city of Ephesus. He told the Corinthians that he would stay there until Pentecost, "for a *wide door* for effective service has opened to me, and there are *many adversaries.*" For 160 years missionaries in Thailand have encountered open doors but closed hearts. The adversaries — occult, superstition and religion — continue to blind Thai people to the light of the gospel.

As furlough approached, both our families felt that the task in Lamnarai was incomplete and one couple would need to return for a second term. The Curtises were selected for this role.

It was providential that the Curtises were based in Pasadena, California for part of that furlough. Their apartment was close to the Center for World Missions and Buzz was able to attend classes there. One course was on spiritual warfare. The more the professor talked about our authority over Satan and the need of extraordinary prayer and fasting to bring down demonic strongholds, the more excited Buzz became. In Lamnarai we both knew spiritual forces were at work, but had never learned to bind them through our authority in Christ. We had expended a great deal of effort, but with little spiritual result.

When Buzz and Ruthi returned to Lamnarai in April 1985 they teamed up with a Thai Bible school graduate and began to implement some of the concepts Buzz had learned on the homeside. The main innovation was a day of prayer and fasting every Wednesday. Besides praying for general needs, the team put special emphasis on binding the demonic forces which were curtailing the advance of the gospel in Lamnarai.

When I got an opportunity to return to Lamnarai, the change was obvious. The church was no longer a simple lean-to with a hot tin roof and crude benches. The believers had purchased a piece of property and erected a stilt house on it. Membership was up to around forty and a committee of five leaders was helping run the church. Buzz and Ruthi worked themselves out of a job, so when their second term ended they handed the church over to national leadership and moved on to begin again elsewhere.

What the Curtises discovered was a fundamental spiritual principle, often overlooked in our method-conscious, activity-minded, high-tech world. Our warfare is not human but is against invisible demonic powers which cannot be touched by fleshly weapons. Jesus said that certain demonic forces come out only through prayer and fasting. The Satanic forces in Thailand are in this category. Only extraordinary and urgent corporate prayer accompanied by fasting can bind these forces and release the power of the Spirit.

The formula for success in spiritual warfare in Thailand is possibly best seen in the following excerpt from *World Christian*[2]: "I remember hearing a retired missionary couple tell of their amazing experiences in Thailand. After a long time with little results they realized that the

[2] Jan/Feb 1985

spirits that held their people were preventing the gospel from having an impact. They set aside one day a week to go out alone in the woods and do nothing but bind the demons and loose God's Spirit. Before long, they saw God begin to heal and change lives in a tangible and powerful way. They eventually experienced a wave of conversions among that people."

What "works" in Thailand? Perhaps it is easier to say what doesn't work. It certainly isn't a particular tract, film, or evangelistic method. What does work are two simple yet overlooked spiritual disciplines — fasting and prayer. If the missionary on the field and supporters back home can learn to apply these two disciplines, surely the "wave of conversions" we have been expecting for over 160 years cannot be far behind.

SIXTEEN

GOD'S MEGAPHONE

God whispers to us in our pleasures,
speaks in our conscience, but shouts in our pains:
it is His megaphone to rouse a deaf world.
(C.S. Lewis — The Problem of Pain)

Yellow Fever ... cholera ... typhoid. I thought the World Health Organization had eradicated those plagues decades ago. Eleven injections at a local clinic in Shawnee were ample proof of their continued presence in Thailand. As new workers we were naive about many things — the chance of getting sick wasn't one of them.

To appreciate the health risk of living in Thailand, consider the historical perspective. In the first twenty years of missionary work in Thailand, before the era of preventive medicine and antibiotics, the average length of service was less than five years — one term. At that time cholera, typhoid, dysentery, smallpox and malaria ravaged the land, especially the swampy central plain. In 1868 Dr Samuel House was traveling to north Thailand to help two missionaries deliver their babies, when he was gored by an elephant. With no help nearby, he decided to sew up the three-inch gash in his abdomen himself, using a hand mirror and no anesthetics. He then instructed his companions to carry him on a stretcher to Chiang Mai. Normally gore wounds were fatal, but Dr House survived and went on to Chiang Mai to help deliver the babies.

During World War II prisoners of war who built the famous "Bridge over the River Kwai" on the Thailand/ Burma border suffered from the three D's: dermatitis, diarrhea, and dementia. The fourth "D" was death. Over 16,000 allied soldiers and 100,000 Asians died constructing the railway.

Since then modern medicine has removed some major plagues like smallpox, but others still remain. Most of these can be traced to Anopheles Culex, the common mosquito. This whining little intruder is the bane of tourists and residents alike. I remember one tourist from England who looked like Job. She was covered from head to toe with red splotches — an allergic reaction to mosquito bites.

Before World War II, houses were not screened. Men had to wear special mosquito boots with leather tops halfway up to the knees. Women used a light cloth bag which they draped over their skirts. Emelie Bradley, wife of Dr Bradley, said that the large Thai mosquito "delighted particularly in the fresh blood of newcomers."

Today we have repellants, creams, gels and coils to fight these pesky insects. Slapping is the most primitive and least effective method, but is widely used. I can usually gauge the number of terms a missionary has had by his skill at slapping mosquitos. The tiny mosquito is remarkably smart. They know to bite near the edge of clothing and are experts at avoiding a sudden slap.

These days we take anti-malarial pills as a preventative. Before they became available, the only drug was quinine. In China, people who professed Christ in order to get food were called "rice Christians." In north Thailand the missionaries dispensed so much quinine that a group of "quinine Christians" or "white medicine Christians" appeared. Malaria gradually became resistant to quinine, and just twenty years ago it was claiming 30,000 lives per year in Thailand.

Taking pills regularly helped me to avoid malaria, but offered no protection from other prevalent fevers. During that first term I came down with glandular, typhoid and dengue fever. During Dr Livingstone's first five-year term in Africa he suffered 31 attacks of fever, which puts mine into perspective. Of the three fevers, dengue, nick-named breakbone fever, was the most widespread. Within three months of our moving up-country, four of the six of us had contracted dengue.

Dengue is borne by the striped day-flying mosquito. Its symptoms include high temperature for four to six days, achy joints, red eyes, and it concludes with a rash. There is no treatment; you must patiently let the fever run its course.

Once when my temperature soared to 104 degrees, Paula lost her patience and decided to act. She instructed me to take a shower and then began to apply towels soaked in iced water to my chest and forehead, as a fan blew full blast on my naked body. As my teeth and body began to shake I wondered if the cure was worse than the fever.

It is bad enough when an adult gets a fever but doubly frightening when your child develops a high tempera-ture. Low grade fevers which rise during the day and subside at night were fairly common. After three to five days of sustained high fever, all missionaries were in-structed to head for Manorom Hospital.

Just two weeks before our departure for furlough, five-year-old Andy developed a fever one Sunday. By Tuesday, he seemed better but was still running a tem-perature. Finally at 10:30 pm on Wednesday he vomited blood. I immediately wrapped him in a blanket, put his limp body on the gas tank of my motorcycle and drove to a local clinic. The doctor refused to open his clinic at that hour; the local hospital was our only alternative. We thought about taking Andy to Manorom but he was too sick to travel.

At the hospital the doctor diagnosed it as hemorrhagic fever, another mosquito-borne fever which causes internal bleeding. The emergency department was busy. Andy watched wide-eyed as a motorcycle crash victim was brought in. The hospital was at capacity, so they put Andy in the hall next to a comatose drunk. I asked for a mosquito net but none could be found.

The only cure was to give glucose intravenously and keep checking his blood count. The nurse pricked his finger on the hour every hour, and when she had finished all ten fingers she started over again. Paula took the day shift and I slept alongside Andy at night Help from the nurses was minimal; relatives were expected to supply food and basic care for the patients. This close interaction provided many opportunities to share Christ with other patients and relatives.

After two days and three bottles of glucose, Andy was released. When we returned home both of us felt physically and emotionally drained. On more than one occasion during the ordeal we had to give Andy back to the Lord in prayer.

As Christians it was natural for us to call on the Lord to help our sick child. It was just as normal for the Thai to call on the spirits. I visited that same hospital with a local Christian. As we entered, we noticed a boy in the last stages of cerebral malaria. My friend stayed and watched as his life slowly ebbed away. After the body was removed, a woman told him that a fierce demon lived in the bed and had killed the boy. She had tried to warn the boy's father but he wouldn't listen. A nurse confirmed that three people had died on that bed in recent months. The woman said, "If you want to sit or lie on this bed, you must ask permission of the demon and place a garland or money on the bed as a peace offering." This was not an isolated incident. The majority of Thai live in fear of offending the spirits.

After the incident with Andy we thought we could "coast" the last week or so before furlough. Not so. One week before our departure date, two-year-old Timmy came down with dengue fever. Paula went off with him to Manorom, thus missing our farewell from the Lamnarai church.

Water-borne diseases are also common. Once at our field conference a number of missionaries became ill with stomach problems. It turned out the drinking water had not been filtered. However, even if you scrupulously filter the water and avoid ice the chances are you will still get diarrhea. So common is this malady that the Thai have four or five picturesque words to describe it, such as walking stomach, broken stomach or running stomach. At one point Paula had it for six weeks. After a few attacks you don't even bother to consult a doctor. After a week with no relief you take a drug called Lomatil. If that doesn't work you probably have an amoeba which calls for Thalazole. Paula found herself taking eight pills a day. At the end of the term I thought about buying stock in Thai pharmaceuticals; missionaries will always keep them in business.

One reason foreigners have stomach problems is the spicy nature of Thai food. It takes a while to get used to Thai curry and other "exotic" dishes. Some you never get used to, like beetle salad, ant eggs, and fried locust. One man announced we would be having frog for dinner.

I said, "Oh good, we eat frog legs all the time back in

Oklahoma."

He replied, "I didn't say frog legs, I said frog — the whole thing." He then cut up a toad in small pieces and placed them in a pot for our evening meal. After a number of similar culinary adventures Buzz began to sing:

"Where He leads, I will follow;
What He feeds me I will swallow."

Once I developed a high temperature and Paula rushed me to the Manorom Hospital. For the next sixteen days a fever caused me to shake, break out in a sweat and chill. Since I didn't have the abdominal pain of classic typhoid, the doctor labeled it walking typhoid. It was true I could walk, but I didn't feel much like strolling around after averaging four hours of sleep each night for two weeks. Paula didn't look much better; she was going through morning sickness for the third time. When my mother heard of our ordeal she wrote back, "I thought typhoid had been wiped off the face of the map years ago."

I feel a special debt to the missionaries at Manorom Hospital. Not only have they nursed my family back to health on numerous occasions; they have also laid a foundation for our outreach in Lamnarai. In central Thailand half of the Christians were first contacted through Manorom, and in the south over 90% of Malay Christians have made commitments to Christ due to the outreach centered at Saiburi Christian Hospital.

At times our family couldn't make it to Manorom. On these occasions, we relied on a manual called *Where There Is No Doctor*. Once I came down with a severe abdominal pain. Paula consulted the manual which indicated an acute appendicitis. Transporting me to Manorom in that condition was out of the question. Paula put the manual aside, laid her hands on my body and began to pray. Within a short time the mysterious pain faded. When I got up from bed I found a blue magic marker and wrote in bold letters under the title, *Where There Is No Doctor* the word "PRAY."

On another occasion I visited a very isolated Christian, Mr Saman. His wife had been experiencing back pain for some time. I didn't have my medical manual, and transporting her to the hospital would have been difficult. Instead I turned to James 5:14-15 concerning prayer for the sick.

I asked Mr Saman, "Do you have any oil?"

"No," he replied, "but would kerosene from this lamp do?"

I took the kerosene, anointing his wife as I prayed for her back. Some time later a beaming Mr Saman described how his wife's back pain went away after we prayed.

Visits from relatives are a special treat for missionaries. We expected my parents' visit in December of 1982 to be a fun-filled time of fellowship and relaxation. The first couple of weeks at the beach met all our expectations. It was during the third week that a near tragedy struck.

We had been in Lamnarai only two days when my father woke up with a bad pain, unable to pass urine. After another twelve hours an OMF doctor advised us to take him to the local hospital. The nurse in emergency informed us that the doctor was out to dinner! As we waited, a suicide and a gunshot victim were admitted. Finally a young doctor, fresh out of medical school, came to examine Dad. When a catheter failed, the doctor advised draining the bladder with a needle. Dad by this time was in great pain and kept asking repeatedly, "What did he say, Larry?" After I described the procedure Dad said, "Ask him if it is risky or not." I turned to the doctor and asked, *"Andarai mai?* — Is it dangerous?"

He replied in broken English, "Oh, it is jus' routine."

After an hour, the doctor finished and charged us $3.50 for his services. He advised us to get Dad to Bangkok as soon as possible for more permanent relief. By this time it was 10 pm and no transportation was available. The doctor assured us that an ambulance would come for us the next morning.

At 4:30 am an attendant drove up in the "ambulance" — a Datsun pickup. We loaded Dad and his sleeping bag, along with another Thai man, into the truck. Thirty minutes later I noticed Dad had curled up with the Thai man to keep warm as we bumped along on the three-and-a-half-hour drive to Bangkok.

A specialist in Bangkok diagnosed Dad's problem and, just days before Christmas, operated on his prostate. On December 27 we rolled him to the airport in a wheelchair for the return trip and further surgery. Later he commented on his experiences: "Despite being in the hospital for an operation I can say that this trip has been one of the most rewarding experiences of my life. I especially enjoyed getting acquainted with my two grandsons and renewing family ties with Larry and Paula. God has put me here to slow down and reflect on life (he read *Born Again* and *Life Sentence* by Chuck Colson while in hospital). In 35 years of married life I have never been in the hospital or seriously ill. I hope I never have to go through those thirty hours of pain ever again. Through it all I've come to appreciate the love and concern of the OMF family."

C S Lewis was right. God often uses pain to rouse our lethargic spirits and awaken us from complacency. David spoke of this in Psalm 119:71, "It is good for me that I was afflicted, that I may learn thy statutes."

In the comparative ease and comfort of America, God

had spoken to our family in a whisper. In Thailand we had the privilege of hearing His voice more clearly through various ailments. They drew us closer as a family and closer to God. We were also drawn closer to the missionary community who sat at our bedside, delivered our baby, listened to our complaints and mended our broken bodies and spirits. My Buddhist friends see suffering as something to be avoided, a weapon wielded indiscriminately by blind fate. But as a Christian I now see, like C S Lewis, that pain is actually a megaphone in the hands of a loving God.

SEVENTEEN

HOUSE OF NEW LIFE

*I began to comprehend, while living with the Aucas,
something of what it means to be a foreigner, to lose one's own
culture for the sake of winning those of another.
I began to appreciate, as I had not appreciated
in six previous years of missionary life, the necessity of removing
as many of the distractions from our message as possible.
(Elisabeth Elliot)*

The principle that Elisabeth Elliot referred to is called
identification. It is the same principle Paul spoke of in I
Corinthians 9:22, "I have become all things to all men,
that I may by all means save some." To the Thai, Christianity is the *farang's* (foreigner's) religion. To remove
this prejudice, we found it necessary to remove some of
our foreign behavior and ideas. Adapting to the local
way of life allowed us to build bridges and break down
barriers, and helped the Thai become more at ease with
us as people and thus more accepting of our message.

Our first houses were similiar to those of other teach-
ers in the neighborhood. At first people dropped by in
droves, but after a year or so the novelty wore off and we
had fewer unexpected guests. Our location was some-
what off the beaten track, and the wear and tear of living
side by side as missionary families was taking its toll. We
began to think that it was time to divide and conquer.

The Curtises had noticed that other missionaries lived in the middle of the market area, and began looking for similiar housing. When their term was cut short, the option to move fell to our family. In the spring of 1983 we began to pray in earnest for an outreach in the market.

Finding a house in Thailand isn't easy. There are no real estate signs or classified ads: you must rely on word of mouth. Soon we heard of a two-story shophouse next to the fresh market.   These unpainted lapped-wood houses measure only 15 by 40 feet, have tin roofs with no ceiling, a single bathroom and no partitions. They share a common wall and are built in domino fashion, one house against another. There is no yard; only a narrow sidewalk separates the occupants from the road.

This former beauty shop was anything but beautiful. The floor was covered with wall-to-wall garbage, old clothing, shoes, mail, paper and worn-out baskets. The kitchen wall was eaten through and the bathroom, made of rusted iron, had no door or vessel to hold water. A broken-down Chinese altar was on the floor, occult symbols covered the walls, and a spirit house stood guard outside.

Paula wrote home, "If you could see it right now, as it is, you would first gag and then die, I know. When my eyes saw it they sent a message to my brain. A double neon sign started flashing ... ''No way! No way! No way!' Yet my spirit was saying, 'This is just what you've been praying for ... a place to rub shoulders with more Thai people.'"

Andy overheard us talking about the house and asked, "What's wrong, Mommy? Is the house broken?"

Paula replied, "No honey, we just want to be closer to our Thai friends so they can learn more about Jesus."

Paula's dad had taught her three principles of real

estate, "Location, location, location." With this in mind we agreed to rent the shophouse. What it lacked in aesthetics it made up for in its central position in the market.

As an interior designer, Paula found it a challenge to turn this "dump" into a habitable dwelling. Her first stipulation was a room with air conditioning. Temperatures under the tin roof upstairs could easily hit 120 degrees. Funds were limited, so Mr Hit volunteered to help me construct a 14 by 14 foot cubicle out of plywood. Next, he and some other Christians removed the spirit shelves, spirit house and other occult paraphernalia. The Chinese landlord had no objections; he was happy to see me fix up the place and knew I would pay the 35 dollars a month rent on time. I asked him if the house ever flooded. He said, "Oh no, don't worry about that." Later I would regret not having that statement written down and notarized.

On June 11, 1983, we dedicated "The House of New Life". Sixty believers who were having a regional meeting at a local school paraded with banners to our new house. Paula and I spread newspaper on the bare floor for them to sit on. We sang some hymns, then Pastor Jarern prayed for God's presence and protection over the house and its occupants. I especially appreciated his prayer binding the forces of Satan which had been associated with the house in the past.

The fresh market outside our door was a combination city hall, shopping mall, playground, newsstand, and theater. Like clockwork, at 5:30 am we were awakened by pork sellers cutting meat on wooden blocks. Soon after this, fruit sellers laid out coconuts, mangos, papaya, mangosteen and rambutan on mats along the narrow lane.

Around six am barefoot monks would walk through

the market in single file begging alms, the oldest at the front with his saffron robe pulled close to his chest against the morning chill. They walked slowly, without expression, from shop to shop, a black begging bowl with a brass lid suspended from their shoulders.

This parade of humanity continued throughout the day. Beggars, traveling minstrels, housewives, officials and children passed our house by the hundreds. Two sides of our corner shop were open to public scrutiny. Often people would stop to read a poster with John 14:6 written in large letters: "I am the way, the truth, and the life; no man comes to the Father but through me."

The atmosphere in the market was definitely Chinese. Around 70% of the market people were of Chinese descent, even though they make up only 10% of the total population. In Thailand, the Thai run the farms and government, while Chinese monopolize the markets. The Thai are more pleasure loving whereas the Chinese are all business. A Thai told me, "If a Chinese gets ten baht, he spends three and saves seven. If a Thai gets ten baht, he spends eleven and goes into debt (usually to the Chinese)." Chinese shops are rarely closed, opening early and closing late seven days a week. The only break is during Chinese New Years.

Although fully assimilated into Thai society, the Chinese still maintain their ancestral worship, family titles and language, especially among the older generation. Once I saw Louis Almond listening to a tape and asked him what it was. "I'm boning up on my Swatow," he said. "You can't really reach the Chinese unless you speak some of their dialect." Louis had been a missionary in China 35 years previously and knew the importance of identifying with the special needs of the Chinese. We found it difficult to share with these highly pragmatic and materialistic merchants. They were interested in immediate solutions and prosperity in this life; the Christian's "pie in the sky" had no real appeal.

Our Chinese next-door neighbor was a diabetic grand-father whose occupation was "renting" amulets and charms. (The word "sell" is considered too demeaning for such sacred objects.) I have never seen a house with a larger spirit shelf. One whole wall was covered with antique Chinese idols, Buddhas, incense and brass offer-ing bowls. *Apa,* as we called him, was not too friendly, but his niece loved our children, struck up a friendship with our housegirl and even attended a few meetings. It was interesting how God placed the House of New Life next to the amulet sales center for Lamnarai.

Across the street was the local photographer. A friend-ship developed after we asked him to take some photos for our family. One day he showed me pictures he had taken of a local Chinese spirit festival. On an elevated platform stood a spirit medium piercing his tongue with a two-foot dagger. Another shot showed the medium walking on hot coals and splashing hot oil over his body without any apparent pain.

The photographer said he was at first skeptical of the medium's power, but was urged by friends to see for himself. The last picture showed our neighbor sitting on the ground as the medium applied hot oil on his bare back. He told me, "At first I thought this was just a show, but now I have proven it myself; the power of that spirit is real." After that incident I found it difficult to share with my photographer friend. He had proven the reality of his god by a test. The invisible God I spoke about had no attraction.

Each morning Mrs Little sold sauteed pork across from our house. She was very friendly and welcomed us to the neighborhood, saying, "I'm so glad to see a Chris-tian teacher come to the market." However, she consistently refused our invitations to attend meetings. Then one day her sixth child, just a few months old, became ill. In desperation Mrs Little turned to Paula for help. Paula found a gaunt and anemic little girl, her face covered with blisters. After praying, she took the baby to a local doctor. He asked, "Mrs Little, what have you been feeding this baby?"

"Well, doctor," she replied, "she hasn't wanted to eat so I've given her sweetened-condensed milk."

The doctor turned to Paula and said in English, "This baby has malnutrition. See to it that she gets proper care and food." Paula bought some food supplements and began visiting regularly. As the baby's health improved, so did Mrs Little's attitude towards the gospel. Gradually over a nine-month period she began to attend meetings and even brought her children, whom she had named according to the English alphabet ... A,B,C, etc. On furlough we got word that Mrs Little had been baptized and incorporated into the church.

Just down from our house was the town brothel. I was told that during peak periods a hundred girls worked this small town. As an ignorant *farang*, I stumbled upon this establishment while witnessing one evening. A group of young men were seated around a table in front of what looked like an ordinary house. I had just started to hand out tracts when the hostess approached me as a "customer". Catching the drift of her words, I made a quick exit. Later a young prostitute who had been exposed to Christianity in the north visited our home. We loaned her some tapes and she even bought some books.

After we had lived in the market for one month the monsoon rains began, and we finally realized why the rent was so cheap. When we came downstairs, the bottom floor was covered ankle deep in black sludge. We didn't even have time to pick up the linoleum. After this happened around ten times, I went back to the landlord.

"Well, actually I wasn't sure if it flooded or not," was his feeble reply.

Once during a thunderstorm Paula was praying with Andy that the house wouldn't flood. Andy added, "Thank you, Lord Jesus, for the nice rain which helps the farmers' fields grow, but please, Jesus, make it stop soon!" I felt the same way — enough was enough. By the time we left the House of New Life   (which we had renamed Noah's Ark) it had flooded eighteen times. After each flood it took around an hour to clean. The boys loved it. It gave them a chance to use the downstairs as a "slippery slide".

On furlough someone asked me if our home had running water. "Yes," I said, "water runs in the back door and right out the front door."

Another problem we faced was rats! We tried everything. We set wire traps, but the rats were so fat they didn't fit through the trap door. They sprung ordinary traps with impunity. We tried poison, but one died under the floorboards and the house stunk for weeks! Our last resort was the "glue" method. The instructions said, "coat a board with glue, place food in the middle and wait." We baited and waited but no rat! We lost whole bars of soap, $15 worth of Tupperware and a plastic trash can. They even ate through the metal screening on the food cabinet.

Paula is able to handle many of the vicissitudes of missionary life — but not rodents! We were leisurely eating our lunch one day when she felt something nibble at her toe. She sprang to her feet and then sat down again. Soon the same rat climbed up the back of her chair, onto her shoulder and into her lap. She let out a bloodcurdling cry and began to jump madly around the room, shaking her clothes. As she passed the dish cabinet her elbow went through the glass door. Andy and Tim sat wide-eyed as their mommy circled the table like an Indian on the warpath. When she finally calmed down Andy asked, "Daddy, is Mommy all right?"

Visitors were a rarity at the House of New Life. Paula's sister Nancy, however, insisted on staying with us up-country. She had just arrived from Singapore where she had stayed at the luxurious Raffles Hotel. The accomodations at our "hotel" were quite different. The night before her departure she developed a fever and felt quite ill. The prospect of being marooned with us sent her into a state of panic. That night she told Paula, "Promise me one thing, sissy. No matter how sick I am tomorrow — GET ME ON THAT PLANE!" She was still feverish as we led her to the van that would take her to Bangkok. The street was muddy and as she got into the van I pointed out her mud-caked shoes. She took them off and tossed them into the street, "You keep 'em, I'm getting out of here."

There were times when we too would have liked to escape. One time, three of the four Dinkins got sick. Our co-workers were going out of town so they called a nurse in a neighboring town to cook, watch the boys and run the household. That night Tim was crying loudly and Andy had just crawled into our bed. Paula, in the throes of morning sickness, could take it no longer. She cried out suddenly, "Why can't we have a *normal* life like other people!"

For the Thai, life in the market was normal, but for us it was the most abnormal existence we had ever encountered. In our saner moments we knew that God had specifically called us to an abnormal lifestyle, yet amid the yearly moves, floods, rats and lack of privacy, we secretly yearned for normalcy.

The main lesson we learned during our time in the

market was what OMF calls "the incarnation principle". In order to communicate the gospel, God became flesh and dwelt among us (John 1:14). Our live-in ministry was an extension of His incarnation. Sorting out just how far identification extends is never easy. Some take it to an extreme. Father Joseph Damien, a Catholic missionary, identified with the outcasts of Hawaiian society to such an extent that he contracted leprosy. Such assimilation is admirable, but I don't believe the missionary must forfeit his or her nationality, heritage or health to achieve it. Even if you go native, the you/me, *farang*/Thai stigma still remains. How far do we identify? As far as it takes to communicate Christ clearly!

> Ada Lum sums it up:
> Eliminate the unnecessary
> Minimize the differences
> Capitalize on the similarities.

I now realize how difficult it is to minister to someone with whom you are not willing to live. Recently I heard Dr Keith Phillips, founder of World Impact, speak at a missions conference. In the late 1960s Dr Phillips tried to minister to a ghetto in the Watts area of Los Angeles by commuting from an upper-class suburb called Woodlawn. He gradually saw the futility of such a long-distance ministry, applied for public housing, and for over twenty years has raised his family in inner-city Watts. Dr Phillips helped me see that to impact a ghetto you must be willing to live in the ghetto. Merely sending financial contributions, cast-off clothing or food baskets at Christmas will not get the job done.

On January 28, 1987, during Chinese New Year, a merchant burning paper money for his dead ancestors set the Lamnarai market on fire. A steady wind fanned the flames and within a short time two hundred houses had been destroyed. The houses of two Christian families in the market were saved at the last moment by fire trucks.

Although we had not lived there for three years, we were concerned for our former neighbors and sought them out. The devastation was worse than I expected. All that was left of the former House of New Life was the charred walls of the bathroom and the twisted metal front door.

I watched as our neighbors sifted through the remains of their family dwellings. Many had fled the flames with only the clothes on their backs, clutching a few precious Buddha images. As we toured the now blackened market, I stopped to talk with one of them.

"You had to save your idols from the fire, didn't you?" I asked him. When he agreed, I said, "Remember, we Christians have a God who saves man, not a god who needs to be saved by man."

EIGHTEEN

MKS — MISSIONARY KIDS

Educating children on the field is probably the greatest single problem that married missionaries face.

The wellbeing and education of children was certainly our greatest concern when we attended the OMF candidate school. Just what provisions did the mission make for MKs? Beyond that, was Asia a suitable and safe place to raise children? This issue struck an emotional chord, especially as Paula was six months pregnant with our first child. During the course, OMF leaders answered our questions and allayed our fears. They were right. Our children proved an asset in our ministry and opened many doors to nonChristians.

The child himself benefits from life overseas. Our children are not "National Geographic Christians". They have seen and tasted many different cultures and climes. They speak a foreign tongue and have seen God at work in various settings. It is true they have been denied some of the amusements of the West, like video games, but I believe that their imagination and creativity have improved in the process. They have not been shielded from the needy and suffering people around them — some of their friends bear the marks of leprosy and poverty.

Another advantage is in the area of family time. Busy

parents in the States have limited family time. For most of the children's waking hours their father is away doing a job the children rarely see or understand. As a missionary, however, my home *is* my office and each family member is an integral part of the ministry.

At first I didn't appreciate this fact. Once I was complaining to John Casto, who had raised five boys on the field, about the seemingly inordinate amount of time it takes to raise a family in Thailand. John said, "Larry, my family was a ministry to the Thai. The way I treated my wife and kids was very important to our overall ministry."

Thai people have a deep affection for children. From birth they are the center of attention in every home. You can imagine their reaction to two fair-haired, blue-eyed toddlers. Andy and Nathan were the main attraction in the market whenever their mothers took them shopping. The Thai called them *dukada,* meaning "doll", and filled them with candy as they competed to hold or talk to them. They got used to being passed around like little pink footballs. A full-page ad in the local newspaper wouldn't have made our presence known as effectively as simply buying vegetables with Andy and Nathan in tow. Visitation always seemed to go better when we took the boys along. They acted as a non-threatening bridge into the businesses and homes of Lamnarai.

We learned quickly, however, that the Thai philosophy of discipline was different from ours. Thai children are treated permissively by western standards. In the early years they have a free reign; later deliberate mischief is disciplined but spanking is rare.

In the market shophouse we made the mistake of spanking our boys in full view of the neighbors. Soon a delegation was sent to inform us of our error. As Buddhists, they felt a child was born innocent and pure; it was the environment that was to blame for the child's sin. As Christians, we believed otherwise. Although we continued to spank our children, we did it secretly so as not to offend.

Once a neighbor was lamenting her inability to control her three year old. She had tried to bribe him with candy but it didn't work. We suggested she try spanking. She said, "Oh no, I couldn't do that. You see, my son knows I'm six months pregnant and has threatened to punch me in the stomach if I smack him."

Although we declined to follow the Thai in discipline, we did respect their wisdom in "potty training". In Thai homes there is no "potty", and the climate makes diapers a liability (unless you enjoy treating heat rash). The Thai method is to put a top on the child (so he won't catch cold) but leave his bottom uncovered. Then follow him around with a towel for "mopping up" operations. I wrote home, "It's sort of like training a puppy, except here we don't put down newspapers." This method worked surprisingly well — until relatives came to visit. We had the hardest time convincing my mother of the advantages of this custom.

Raising a child in Asia will stretch even the most patient parent. Tim recognized this in one of his prayers at lunch. After a particularly hectic morning Paula asked Tim if he would like to bless the food. After his regular circuit of family, pets, and friends he ended the prayer with, "And Jesus, please help Mommy not to go crazy."

Tim is learning a lot. He now knows that Jesus is the A to Z, not the A to B. He also knows all about the Lord's Supper. At church, the pastor substituted small balls of sticky rice for the communion bread. Tim kept asking if he could eat the elements along with the others. I told him, "No Tim, you can't eat of the Lord's Supper until you've trusted Jesus, and you can't get to heaven by eating bread anyway." Tim shot back, "Well, you can if you eat sticky rice!"

Paula is from a family of seven and always wanted a large family. It was during our first year of language study that she began to show the familiar signs of nausea and vomiting. The Thai expression for "pregnant" is *mee tong* (You have a stomach). Sure enough, Paula did indeed have a "stomach" due in February of 1982. The three Dinkins bears — pappa, momma, and baby — were about to become four.

Pregnancy is always difficult, especially in the tropics. Paula spent a third of our term popping avomine pills, swelling at the ankles and eating strange combinations of Thai food. Prenatal checks at home were just across town, here they were an eight-hour round-trip by bus. Having to watch children and do language study didn't help either. Once when Paula was a few weeks pregnant, Andy entered the house holding a present for Mommy by the tail — barbecued rat! The next thing I heard was Paula closing the bathroom door briskly behind her.

Eventually the morning sickness passed and it was time to move to Manorom to await delivery. In my estimation, Manorom is to birthing what Mayo Clinic is to research. Visitors stay in a nearby guest house where meals are prepared and clothes laundered. There are toys and playmates for the children, a library and prayer meetings for adults. They even have sports facilities, sightseeing trips and a fine church in the market.

Paula's parents arrived a couple of weeks early for the big occasion. As we waited, Paula caught a tummy bug and was hospitalized two days, and Andy recovered from the measles. The due date came and went with no action on Paula's part.

On February 10, Paula went into labor. In Oklahoma we had taken Lamaze classes, and through Andy's birth had become used to coordinating the fetal monitor with breathing techniques. Here there was no monitor; a trumpet-shaped device dating back to Thomas Edison's era was placed on the womb in order to check the baby's heartbeat. The nurse checked contractions by putting her hand on Paula's stomach while she filled in squares on what looked like a crossword puzzle. In the States I had led Paula in "pyramid breathing", but here all our techniques went out the window.

In labor rooms back in the States you often hear screams and harsh language. This labor room was strangely quiet. The nurse explained that Thai women have a high threshhold of pain and are very good to work with. I knew what she meant. Once I saw two very pregnant Thai women sitting on a hard bench waiting for what I presumed was a prenatal check. I asked if they were waiting to see the doctor. The nurse said, "No, they're both in labor. They are waiting their turn to deliver!"

Thai men, on the other hand, aren't as tough as their wives. Every time I see Thai men waiting outside the delivery room, I encourage them to go in, support their wife and witness the miracle of birth. So far I have had no takers. One told me, "Oh, I don't want to go in there, there might be blood."

We had been buying pink dresses in anticipation of Amy Elizabeth but the nurse announced it was an eight pound eight ounce boy — Timothy Merle. Paula shared a room with six other mothers and all their relatives. The relatives are there to provide food and other assistance since there is no "room service". I shoved a mattress under Paula's bed and acted as nurse for the first day or so.

Tim was quite a sensation on the ward and people were constantly opening the crib to get a peek. The excitement abated, however, when I threatened to charge an admission fee to see this unusual creature. Even with the inconveniences, at least the price was right — $60 for everything.

When you have a child in the States you take many things for granted — like birth certificates. At home all the paper work is done for you, but here it is the parents' responsibility. The first step was to secure US citizenship for Tim. I arrived at the embassy near closing time on Friday to fill out forms. When I deposited the forms and translations on the desk the clerk said, "That will be $35 dollars, please." All I had was $20! The clerk said I would have to return on Monday, but we were scheduled for a two-week holiday starting Saturday.

A total stranger overheard the conversation and said to me, "Here is $25, take it." At first I declined, and then realized that this was God's provision. I never saw the lady again and she refused to let me pay her back. I am now convinced that God assigns angels to foreign embassies to help forgetful missionaries.

During our time at Manorom we got used to people ogling over our new son, "What a cutie pie ... that is such a sweet baby ..." But when we arrived in Lamnarai the Thai would hold Tim a moment and say, "What an ugly child this is ... he needs a good smack." At first I wanted to say, "My kid's ugly ... huh? Listen lady, your baby isn't exactly Miss Thailand, you know." That was before I understood the superstitious nature of the Thai. Many Thai believe that if you compliment a baby too much the spirits will become interested in it and want to possess it. In order to fool the spirits they say just the opposite of what they really think.

As missionaries we had to get used to these insult-compliments. After we brought blue-eyed, blond-haired Tim home from the hospital, a neighbor commented, "Too bad he's so pale. He'd look so much cuter with black eyes and hair." Once Paula was trying to make friends with a Thai teenager. The girl told Paula, "You're sure getting fat, aren't you!" Believe it or not, she intended it as a compliment. The Thai sometimes use the term "fat" to mean well fed or healthy. In their minds a chubby person is more apt to have good health than a skinny one.

The Thai love to pinch the chubby cheeks of children — especially *farang* children. Andy, at two years, had long red curls in tight ringlets around his head. Anytime we took him out in his stroller he was swarmed by admirers who tried to pinch his pink cheeks. My father-in-law, Ed Robison, observed this for a couple of weeks and finally could take it no longer. Ed was pushing Andy down a sidewalk in Bangkok when two fashionable Thai ladies approached, and as expected started to grab Andy's cheeks. On an impulse Ed grabbed the cheek of one of the ladies and squeezed! The woman was visibly shocked. I asked Ed why he would do such a thing. "I'm getting tired of these folks always pinching my grandbabies!" he replied.

As Andy began to grow, we had to make plans for his education. We had three options: home schooling, boarding school or a national school. In Lamnarai the kindergarten near our house had a good reputation, so we decided to send Andy, and Nathan Curtis, to that school. We prayed that this contact would open doors to the community and help the boys adjust to Thai culture and language. Each morning we dressed Andy in his uniform: white shirt with his name "Yindee" (happiness) on the pocket, red shorts, white socks with patent leather shoes and a black satchel. We sent the boys a bit late in order to miss Buddhist prayers, and then they spent the rest of the morning learning the Thai alphabet, songs, games and hand work.

The highlight of the term was a recital. Andy participated in a Thai version of the "bunny hop" complete with a pink suit and floppy ears. The bunny hop turned into a comedy routine when a plump Chinese bunny hopped in the wrong direction scattering the other bunnies in his path.

Sending Andy to a Thai kindergarten was relatively easy compared with the next step — boarding school. For most this conjures up an image of some reform school right out of Dickens. On furlough, well-meaning parents stuffed our hands with books on home schooling and claimed it as the answer to all our children's academic needs. One couple even offered to raise our kids for us — anything to spare them from boarding school.

When I shared our plans with my pastor in the States he had a hard time accepting the idea. I tried to tell him that Jesus Himself allowed for parents and children to be separated for the gospel's sake.

He replied, "I don't believe there is such a verse in the Bible, show me."

I then turned to Mark 10:29,30, "I tell you the truth, no one who has left home or brothers or sisters or mother or father or *children* or fields for me and the gospel will fail to receive a hundred times as much in this present age (homes, brothers, sisters, mothers, children and fields — and with them, persecutions) and in the age to come, eternal life."

For us, accepting the need for boarding school was made easier by working for three years with Ruthi Curtis. Ruthi was a wonderful testimony to God's watch care over MKs. Her first seven years were spent in north Thailand in a Hmong tribal village. Later she attended boarding schools in Malaysia and the US. Ruthi gave us a realistic picture of what to expect. Yes, separation was painful, but overall it was a positive experience. So positive, in fact, that she was willing to send her son Nathan through the same system. Ruthi's enthusiasm for the mission school and her explanations of life there helped quiet our fears and made us confident that this was where we should send Andy.

Those who have yet to interact with MKs or visit a boarding school are bound to have misgivings about the system. What they don't realize is that the missionary who opts for the mission school is not abandoning his child but is in fact providing for his basic needs in an atmosphere of love and care. The separation is actually harder on parents than children. Often mothers comment to Paula, "You must be so brave to send your children away to a boarding school so young. I could never do that." If they only knew the trial it is for my wife, they would probably rephrase this statement.

We are neither brave nor spiritual when we say goodbye at Bangkok airport each August and February. It is a heart-wrenching experience, but we feel a necessary one. We know that our children will be cared for by a competent and caring staff of Christians who will provide a high level of education. Socially they will be able to mix with children of their own age, language, and culture. Spiritually they will be trained in the Scriptures, Bible memory and devotions. Physically, the boarding school is also healthier. While in Thailand, Andy twice came down with hemorrhagic fever and was hospitalized. Since moving to the cool, 5,000-foot altitude of Malaysia Andy's health has improved with no recurrence of the fever.

Alice Taylor, missionary to China and mother of the present General Director of OMF, Dr James Taylor, was separated from her children for four years during World War II. During that difficult time the Lord gave her a promise, "If you take care of the things dear to God, He will take care of the things dear to you." Resting on that promise, she gave herself to evangelism and Bible teaching in west China while her children were confined to a camp on the eastern coast. At the end of the war the family was reunited.

That same promise is applicable for thousands of missionary families today. To reach the lost around the world, brief separations may be necessary. God as a caring Father is able to ease the pain of separation and watch over MKs in the interim. That which we once viewed as a major hangup to our service in Asia is turning into a blessing and is helping to further the spread of the gospel in Thailand.

NINETEEN

GOOD SENSE OF HUMOR, BAD SENSE OF SMELL

*A sense of humor reveals a sense of balance and proportion.
Are we able to laugh at ourselves?
Can we keep failure in perspective because we know
there is much more to life? Humor is a gift from God
that all missionaries must take to the field.
(Ada Lum)[1]*

*A cheerful heart does good like medicine.
(Prov.17:22, TLB)*

Sharing the gospel in a land where the majority are on the road to a Christless eternity is a serious and sober calling. I do not want to downplay the grave nature of the spiritual battle for men's souls. At the same time, I have observed that those missionaries who are unable to laugh at themselves or giggle along with others don't usually last. Even if they stay on the field, their grave and gloomy disposition causes them to become humorless, pessimistic and critical. I count myself fortunate to have married a woman with a sensitive funny bone. It was no mistake that Paula's senior class gave her the "best sense of humor" award. A wise professor once said, "Take God

---

[1]A Hitchhikers Guide to Missions, p.92 IV Press 1984 Downers Grove, IL

seriously, but yourself not at all."

If there ever was a "saving grace" or life vest for the missionary, it would have to be a sense of humor. A Swede was told by friends not to return to India. "Man," he was urged, "it is 120 degrees in the shade!"

"Vell," said the Swede, "ve don't always have to stay in the shade do ve?"

Sad to say, the standard books on missionary life and work tend to overlook the importance of such a sense of humor. OMF's famous *Principles and Practice* covers all the major aspects of life on the field but fails to include even a paragraph on the place of humor. Some experiences we had in Thailand were comic, others embarrassing; both kinds served to relax tension and lighten the load.

Those who came to a more primitive Siam in the nineteenth century no doubt needed an extra portion of humor to cope with the vicissitudes of life. A Mrs Perkins was riding to a reception in her honor, dressed in her finest white dress. As she rounded a corner her horse tripped and threw her into a buffalo wallow. I could identify with her after another cyclist clipped me on the left as I rounded a corner on my motorcycle one day. I went sliding down the asphalt on my stomach.

Accidents like this are so common that the Thai have coined the phrase *wad thanon* meaning "he's taking road measurements". Thailand is called the "Land of Smiles" and the Thai are apt to smile whether the incident is humorous or tragic. I looked up that day to see four or five carpenters working on a nearby building who were laughing so much at this *farang* measuring the road that they had to hold on to the scaffolding to keep from falling off.

Every parent looks forward to his child's first words. Even if the "dadda" or "mamma" isn't too clear, it brings great delight to the parents. You can imagine how we felt when Andy's second word came out *jing jok*. The *jing jok* or gecko is a three-inch lizard found in every Thai home. This amazing creature has a lightning tongue, suction cup toes and a detachable tail. My boys loved to grab its tail and watch it twitch madly as the other half made a quick getaway. The boys' other pastime was flicking geckos off the window screens, a game they called "gecko astronauts".

Some are endeared to the little creatures, probably because they consume their weight in mosquitos daily. We saw T-shirts which read, "Have you hugged your gecko today?" But to others they are a nuisance, especially when they crawl into your coke bottle, get squished in the door jamb, or worse yet when they or their droppings land on your head. One new missionary was in the bathroom when she felt something land on her nose. Thinking it was an insect, she instinctively slapped at it — a grave mistake. It took three shampoo rinses to remove the gooey mess from her hair. A short time later the same thing happened again — this time at a ladies prayer meeting!

Geckos often turn up in the most unusual places. To a gecko a toaster seems like a perfectly good home until some hapless mishy shoves a piece of toast into its nest. Even the ceiling isn't safe. Becky Leighton was once steaming some noodles for dinner. When she opened the lid, a blast of steam hit a gecko which happened to be above the stove. The poor creature did a back flip into the noodles ... spaghetti a la gecko.

Practical jokers keep missionary life from becoming monotonous. Dr John Toop at Manorom Hospital was known to liven things up from time to time. He once invited a group of medical colleagues to his home for a meal. Before dinner he spread a thin layer of talcum powder on the ceiling above the table. The guests spent the rest of the meal picking geckos out of their water glasses, plates and bowls!

Practical jokes are funny until one happens to you. At language school we used to eat snacks during breaks. Once, an OMFer from Malaysia showed me a white substance in her handkerchief which she described as a Thai candy. It looked so good I took a bite — it was chalk! On another occasion a Thai friend offered me a pod with seeds in it. To be polite I took out one of the seeds and bit into it. The seed was horribly bitter but I tried to smile as I chewed and with some effort swallowed it. Watching my face contort, my friend said, "Don't eat the whole seed, silly — just the cover!"

I've learned that being polite in Thailand can get you in real trouble. A few days after we moved to Lamnarai a girl brought us some "delicacies" to try. In her basket was a pile of fresh frog skins. We let her fry them on our stove and then she offered us some, asking us how we liked them. To be nice I said, "These are great, they kind of remind me of potato chips." This was all our friend needed to hear. For the next few days she brought us "frog chips" by the dozen. At the end of that week she had a new nickname, "frog lady".

Thai and American palates are indeed different. Our Thai dogs seemed to love the rice slop we fed them every day. Buzz's dad, however, thought that Rolly and Tang might like a treat from the States. He sent two dog treats which looked and smelled like genuine beef jerky. The ads said any dog would go crazy for it. Obviously the makers hadn't met Rolly and Tang. They wouldn't touch it. To fool them Buzz cut the treats into fine pieces and hid them in the rice gruel they loved so much.

A second quality required of a missionary is a bad sense of smell. During our year-long stay in the not-so-fresh market, our noses were assaulted by a plethora of odors. Incense burning on spirit shelves mingled with cloves of fresh garlic. Scented steam from noodles burning on a vendor's cart blended with the pervasive odor of rotting vegetables. Possibly the strongest smell came from peppers frying on a Chinese wok. This Thai form of chemical warfare would not only sting your eyes but could curl your hair and clean your sinuses at the same time!

Next to peppers the strongest odor we encountered came from a prickly fruit the size of a football, called durian. Durian's outer ring is covered by *duri,* or sharp thorns. Inside is the edible yellow pulp which emits the odor most foreigners find so offensive. One writer said, "Durian smells like a garbage truck running over a skunk on a damp day... Durian is to fruit what Limburger is to cheese. This fruit is so smelly it is banned from airplanes, trains and many hotels in S E Asia. Despite its odor durian has a delicate sweet taste which some describe as 'butter flavored with almonds'."

One day our neighbor detected an odor and warned us that we had a gas leak. A careful check of our butane stove revealed nothing, and yet the smell persisted. Later in the day, our neighbor returned. "Don't worry, I found the source of our 'gas leak.' It's just my relatives eating durian in the back room."

The longer you stay in a country, the more you adjust to the smells, food, customs, and celebrations. One festival which we could never quite adjust to was Songran, a water-throwing festival held every April 13th, during the hot season. Anything that walks the street is fair game and is sure to get a soaking. Foreigners are a special target and the Thai love to "get a *farang*".

Once I was pushing Andy past a dozen teenagers, all with water containers at ready. I pleaded with them to spare our lives, but as we passed I was soaked with scented water which clouded my glasses. I thought Andy had emerged unscathed but I was wrong. They had smeared his face with liquid powder, which made him look like Casper the friendly ghost.

Paula made the mistake of taking Andy on the back of her bike at Songran. On her way home she had to run the gauntlet between two rows of young people. Instead of returning home in her soaking clothes she decided to pedal for a few extra minutes and, sure enough, she was "drip dry" by the time she arrived home.

Our language supervisor, Dorothy Mainhood, was walking to a dinner party for her fiftieth birthday. Suddenly a crowd of teenagers with water containers cornered her. Dorothy pleaded with them in her most eloquent Thai to spare her nice clothes, but to no avail. She went to the party a wet rag.

In fashion-conscious Bangkok, the style and condition of your wardrobe are quite important, but up-country it is another story. Jokes about the missionary barrel probably originated with up-country missionaries. These are the ones who arrive home for furlough wearing horn-rimmed glasses, low heels, thin ties, and white shoes. The bane of my wife's existence was my footwear. My most comfortable shoes were a pair of 75-cent foam sandals or flip-flops. I did everything from preach to ride motorbikes in those shoes. Paula would say, "Larry, why don't you get some normal shoes like everybody else?"

I'd say, "They're comfortable, and furthermore my senior missionary, Ian, wears them — case dismissed!"

A fellow missionary working with the Yao tribe loved her flip-flops too. She broke the strap on one while on holiday, and instead of purchasing a new pair for 75 cents, she bought a new strap for twenty cents. The only problem was that the new strap was green and the old one, red. We were quite amused to see her at the airport in Bangkok sending her children off to school, still wearing the same mismatched flip-flops.

Actually, it doesn't pay to wear nice clothes upcountry. One day I was speaking with a lady who was holding her small son on her hip. Suddenly, I felt something warm running down my pants leg. No, it wasn't raining! I wanted to say, "Lady, do you think you could point your son in a different direction?" I did finish the conversation — at a distance.

Children probably produce the most embarrassing moments on the field. When Buzz and Ruthi were in Bangkok, they accidentally left the front gate open. Two neighbor children came to visit Nathan, and he showed them upstairs just as Buzz and Ruthi were completing their bath. The two children made a quick bow and said "excuse me" as they bolted out the front gate.

I can handle Thai children fairly well; it is my own children that drive me up the wall. Especially when they pull my newly shot film from the canister (*for the third time!*), deadbolt themselves in the bathroom, or pour the contents of their potty all over the dog.

Lois Fietje can identify with us; she too has four children. One day the children were misbehaving and Lois found herself yelling at them. Later in the day she told them that she wanted to apologize for yelling. Twelve-year-old Bethany spoke up, "That's OK Mom, you and Dad are faithful missionaries to Thailand. Sometimes even faithful missionaries have bad days."

Dr Rachel Hillier told me how a rather bad day started for her. Early one morning she poured a cup of coffee before starting her quiet time. In the darkness she failed to notice something floating in her cup. Half the cup was gone by the time she saw its contents — a dead frog!

It's easy to have a "bad day", especially with newborns. At breakfast one morning, I noticed that Buzz had something white protruding from his ears. I asked what it was, and he explained that when Nathan's crying reached a certain decibel level, he pushed cotton in his ears to keep his sanity.

Once Ruth Adams noticed an elderly lady had something green stuffed in her ears, but it wasn't cotton, it was a leaf! Ruth had been trying to talk to this lady but without response. The relatives kept saying, "Speak up, she's hard of hearing." Then Ruth noticed the leaf, which a herbal medicine doctor had prescribed to cure her deafness.

You see a lot of strange things in Thailand. After church one Sunday I was asked to make change from the offering. I didn't mind that; what made me mad were those who made change as the plate was still being passed! Mr Yen, a fellow pastor, said, "That's nothing, at my church Mrs New pours out the entire offering on the floor and then sifts through the coins before passing it on."

Pastor Jarern often called on me to handle financial matters. Once a Christian leprosy sufferer came to Jarern asking him to change some coins into bills.

Jarern said, "Sure, how much?"

"1300 baht," the leprosy sufferer replied. That was the monthly wage we paid our housegirl!

Jarern asked, "How did you ever get so much money?"

The man said, "I sat down by the Buddhist temple for a couple of days during a festival, stuck out my cup and they kept pouring the coins in."

Neither the beggar nor Jarern wanted to go to the bank, so they elected me as courier. I put the coins in a shoulder bag and started off on my motorbike, which almost tipped over from the weight. As I poured out the

1300 coins I expected the clerk to ask what arcade I had robbed, but as a polite Thai he counted the coins without saying a word.

Faces are another area of confusion. It is hard enough in the West to connect a name with a face, but doubly hard when all faces look the same and are connected to weird-sounding names. My first year all Thai looked alike. A common joke in missionary circles went something like this:

Mishy A: "Do you know Mr Narong?"

Mishy B: "The name rings a bell, but I'm not sure. Can you describe him?"

Mishy A: "Yes, he is about 5'5" tall, thin, with a flat nose, dark eyes and straight black hair."

The above description could fit almost any adult Thai in the country!

It was comforting to realize that the Thai have a similiar problem with *farangs;* we all look alike — tall, long nose, light skin and hair. Once I was in a mess line at a camp, when an elderly Thai granny addressed me as the main speaker, Dr Henry Breidenthal. She said, "I'm sorry, I could have sworn you were Dr Henry; you've got the same curly hair." Our hair may be curly, but Henry wears glasses and is at least twenty years my senior!

In seminary, I remember seeing a book on the humor of Jesus. At first I was skeptical. As I read this book, however, I saw that Jesus as hundred percent man did have a lighter side, and interjected humor at appropriate points in His ministry. Living with impetuous Peter, the sons of thunder, doubting Thomas and the others must have brought a smile to the Savior's lips, if not a belly laugh at times. It may be that we need to add a tenth beatitude to the original nine: Blessed are those who can laugh at themselves, for they shall be kept sane in the serious battles of life.

TWENTY

DO MISSIONARIES HAVE HALOES?

Wings are an elusive fancy. Some may possess them, but they are not very visible, and as for me, there isn't the least sign of a feather. Don't imagine that by crossing the sea and landing on a foreign shore and learning a foreign lingo you "burst the bonds of outer sin and hatch yourself a cherubim".
(Amy Carmichael)

As a youth I placed missionaries on a pedestal. To me a missionary was a man who lived in the jungle, wore a khaki-colored safari suit and a pith helmet, and carried a machete in one hand and a Bible in the other as he sacrificed life and limb to reach some pagan tribe. Spiritually, missionaries were giants, living on a higher plane, unaffected by the lusts and trials of lesser mortals.

Now I know different. Missionaries have no hidden halos. A term in Thailand was sufficient to remove them from their pedestal. Moving to a foreign land didn't save them from marital counseling or psychological treatment. More than one was asked to leave after only one year on the field. One mother admitted to her peers, "At best I am a carnal Christian." In James' words, missionaries are "men of like passion" who have idiosyncrasies and blind spots like the rest of mankind. Missionaries have been known to crack up physically, spiritually and morally. They can be touchy, competitive, irrational, and downright hostile.

The Word of God is unashamedly honest about the weaknesses and blind spots of Bible characters. The conduct of missionaries sent out by the early church was not always above board or Spirit filled. The New Testament records accurately Mark's desertion, Barnabas and Paul's split, Peter's hypocrisy and Timothy's fear. Yet people still insist on placing modern missionaries on a pedestal and act surprised when they fall. Why is this? Perhaps we ourselves fuel the myth by giving less than accurate portrayals of ourselves and our ministry. We tend to downplay personal failures and defeats in order to emphasize victories and conversions. Why does this happen? Some of us find it hard to be transparent concerning our failings while others fear losing support from churches back home.

Isobel Kuhn sailed for China in 1928 with a group of ten young women. An experienced missionary, Ruth Paxson, agreed to teach them the Bible for one hour each day during the voyage. Isobel said that one sentence stood out from Miss Paxson's teaching, "Girls, when you get to China, all the *scum* of your nature will rise to the top." Scum? Isobel was shocked. The ten girls were all fine Christians and nice girls: how could she use the word *scum*? After working in China a brief time she wrote, "I was totally unprepared for the revolt of the flesh that was waiting me on China's shores." The day would come when Isobel got on her knees and admitted, "Lord, *scum* is the only word to describe me."

Ruth Paxson in her book, *Life on the Highest Plane*, describes the process which caused Isobel to eventually see her true self. She wrote: "Let us put this best product of the flesh to the test. Let us take it from a home in which love reigned and sweet companionship was its daily portion, where books lined the library shelves, beautiful pictures adorned the walls, snow white linen covered the table, and from a community life that offered everything to satisfy the intellectual, social, aesthetic and spiritual desires and needs. Transplant this life to an inferior village on the mission field to live within a house with several people of varying temperaments and tastes, with limited household appointments, with untaught, untrained servants, with nothing upon which to rest the eye but mud walls and dirty narrow streets, surrounded by jarring voices and unpleasant odors, and a furlough seven years off — would this best product of the flesh stand the test and come off more than conqueror?"

I can answer her question with one word — NO. Missionary service yanked the halos from our heads, and exposed our fleshly nature. After one stressful upcountry trip, Paula wrote home, "Both of us sense that the Lord is using this time to knock off our rough edges. OUCH! I've never seen so much 'yuk' come out of me." She was unprepared for the exposure of pride, lack of discipline and jealousy which lay concealed in her heart. Someone has said, "The field must work on the missionary before the missionary can work on the field." Another expressed it this way, "God must convert the missionary before he can convert the heathen."

On furlough, I always cringed when a well-meaning church member greeted me with, "Oh honey, you're so brave and self sacrificing. We're so proud of you." I wanted to say, "Listen lady, you've got me all wrong. I'm not particularly brave or self sacrificing. If you could have seen me at different times this last term you might not be so proud either."

I've heard people comment, "That suit certainly brings out the best in him." I've yet to hear someone say that concerning the mission field. When I was placed in the mission cauldron, I noticed that what was appearing on the surface was more dross than gold. What I carefully hid from others at home was brought painfully to light on the field. Many of my peers had the same experience. For most, this is more painful than either culture shock or language shock. It's called self-awareness shock.

Once I was on a committee which analyzed why two missionaries left the field after just one year of service. It wasn't cultural adjustments or language problems which did them in. The main problem was an identity crisis.

We saw Andy go through an identity crisis at the tender age of four. At the time he was one of two white students in a Thai kindergarten. The Thai kids taunted Andy with the word *farang* — foreigner. One day he came home, threw his satchel on the kitchen table and asked, "Mommy, I'm a Thai boy, right?"

Paula replied, "No, Andy, you're a *farang.*"

Andy shot back, "Mommy, that's not true, I know I'm a Thai boy!"

"Andy ... you are a foreign boy, not Thai."

Andy was adamant, "Well, what about Daddy, he's Thai isn't he?"

Paula answered, "No, Daddy is a *farang* too."

"Well, what about you, Mom? You have black hair, that means you're Thai, right?" (Andy didn't ask about his tow-headed, blue-eyed brother, Timmy — that was too obvious).

"No, I'm a *farang* too," replied Mother.

Andy was looking for the answer to the question, "Who am I?" He so wanted to be like the rest of the kids, but just didn't seem to fit in. It wasn't just Andy who was undergoing an identity crisis; all of us to a greater or lesser degree experienced self-awareness shock. The more extreme cases, however, learned that the mission field is not the place to "find yourself" or answer the question,

"Who am I?"

I've learned that self-esteem is a fragile entity and easily shattered. Those who desire to do mission work should discover who they are and develop a confident self-image before ever boarding a plane for overseas. As a missionary you can expect your self-esteem to take an enormous beating. But if you know who you are in Christ, accepted in the beloved and righteous in His sight, your self-image may be scarred in battle, but never shattered.

My early impressions of the mission field came from reading nineteen-century missionary biographies. Little was said about the missionary's personal struggles; instead they stressed heroic efforts to win the heathen against tremendous odds. I was amazed how Hudson Taylor, for example, emerged victorious over robbery, sickness, lack of finances, and persecution.

Yet when I read a more recent biography, *Hudson Taylor and Maria*, I got a totally different impression of the missionary community. I was amazed to find that Hudson's main problem was with his fellow missionaries, not the Chinese! When he adopted Chinese clothes, shaved his head and wore a "pigtail", he was ostracized by fellow missionaries. To top it off, his proposal to Maria Dyer almost caused a riot on the mission compound.

When you talk to missionaries today you will find a similar scenario. One very common cause of missionary dropouts is not the culture, nationals, or living conditions but interpersonal problems with other missionaries. A fellow worker once told Paula, "Once I was having a hard time getting along with so and so — we really clashed."

"How is it now?" Paula asked.

"Oh, we get along splendidly now."

Paula was curious, "Why, what happened?"

"She is back in the States and I'm here!"

For three years we worked closely with the Curtis family. Our friendship started in candidate school and continued to grow through orientation in Singapore and language study in Bangkok. It was natural for us to team up for work in Lamnarai. Overall we were very compatible and got along splendidly. We never had a doctrinal problem or disagreement over the basic philosophy of ministry. What little friction we did experience was in the area of relationships.

First of all we were a very diverse team: including a banker, artist, MK and home economist. Buzz and Ruthi were Baptists, had lived in various countries, including Thailand, and had learned a foreign tongue. Paula and I came from a Methodist background, had only taken tourist trips overseas, and were monolingual.

In Lamnarai we lived in identical houses separated by only a few feet. Our bedrooms were so close that when I sneezed Buzz would say "*gesundheit!*" If church members came to visit one family and not the other, it was easy to feel slighted. As the only foreign couples in town, comparisons were inevitable. People would ask Paula why she didn't speak as well as Ruthi — hadn't they spent an equal length of time in Thailand? Near the end of the term Paula became pregnant with our third child. In the meantime, Ruthi went through the disappointment of two miscarriages. When Paula and Ruthi went on visitation together people would ask, "When are you going to have a baby like Paula, Ruthi?"

Having two toddler boys born within a week of each other brought tension as well. Andy and Nathan thought they were brothers and fought like them too. As parents we found it hard not to compare or measure one against the other.

No one needed to tell me I was a competitive person. I accepted that fact before coming to Thailand. What surprised me was the depth of that competitive streak. Usually I would be pleased with the advances made by others. But on the field I found it hard to "rejoice with those who rejoice," especially when they made better grades in language or got a position I coveted.

Buzz and Ruthi were asked to act as youth sponsors in a neighboring town. I felt slighted: *Why didn't they ask me?* Instead of rejoicing I became jealous and mad. This ungodly attitude began to affect my relationship with my coworkers. It was humbling to have to confess and ask forgiveness. Self-awareness is painful but it does allow God to remove the scum of otherwise-hidden sins.

Life in Thailand was like sailing a boat in a rough sea. One moment we were on the crest of joy, the next moment in a slough of despair. While in one such quagmire, I was asked to produce a slide-tape for a supporting church. I selected the most exciting shots and tried to write a corresponding script. Unfortunately my narration didn't fit the up-beat nature of the slides. After viewing it, the pastor wrote back, "I sensed a real discouragement in your voice." My voice had betrayed the state of my soul.

Feelings of disillusionment aren't unusual for first termers. Hudson Taylor, during his first year in China wrote these words, "I have felt a nervousness since we were so roughly treated in Tungchow which is quite a new experience, a feeling that is not lessened by being quite alone. I could not help feeling sad and downcast." J O Fraser, apostle to the Lisu tribe, also had fits of depression during his first term. His biography, *Mountain Rain*, records:

"Fraser moved to a village called Little River. No one was interested in spiritual things. With the steady downpour of the rain, his clothes sodden, depression began to seep into his very marrow. 'Does God care?' he asked. 'Has He forgotten me? I hoped for great results among these people and ... nothing.'

"The depression deepened until all seemed black and it was an effort to even move. Did I mistake my calling? Five years in China ... What do I have to show for it? Why continue to pray for the Lisu?

"Then, not once but over and over, thoughts of sui-cide plagued Fraser. 'Why go on? I'm so alone. Why struggle to stay alive? It would be so easy to lie on my mat and not eat —just sleep. So easy to misstep on the trail ... go crashing headlong ... In a matter of minutes it would be over'."

Fraser eventually realized the depression was satanic and fought it. Like Fraser, we constantly had to remind ourselves that our fight was not against flesh and blood, but was primarily a spiritual battle. Martin Luther once threw an inkwell at Satan. Since there were no inkwells in Thailand, Paula used words instead. I often observed her hurling Scripture verses and verbal rebukes at the devil as she went about doing her daily chores.

Another lesson we learned concerns the difference between grumbling and groaning. To groan under trial is a natural reation to life in a fallen world. J V McGee maintains that it is also biblical, "we ourselves *groan* ... waiting eagerly our adoption as sons" (Rom 8:23).

Grumbling, on the other hand, is not biblical. One night I returned from a trip, only to be met with a barrage of complaints. Paula ended her verbal broad-side with, "Larry, I feel just like Jeremiah in the cistern."

It was fitting she mentioned Jeremiah. If anyone ever had the right to complain it was the weeping prophet. That is what makes his statement in Lamentations 3: 39 all the more convicting, "Why should any living mortal, or any man, offer *complaint* in view of his sins?" Most of the things Paula mentioned were beyond our control: food, floods, working conditions and sick babies. Murmuring against circumstances outside our control was in effect complaining against God. God is sympathetic to moaning but not murmuring. "Now the people complained about their hardships in the hearing of the Lord, and when he heard them his anger was aroused. Then fire from the Lord burned among them ..." (Numbers 11:1).

Paula's Sunday school teacher, Wilda Mathews, was one missionary who learned to accept adverse circumstances without questioning or muttering. Once while in China Wilda was faced with separation from her husband. She wrote, "One night I lay pleading with the Lord to let us go together, but the next morning I was confronted with Romans 9:20,21: 'Who art thou that repliest against God?' (Or as the margin says, 'disputest with God'.) 'Hath not the Potter power over the clay?' As I faced it squarely, all I could do was to bow my heart and head and say, 'not my will but thine be done.'" Wilda's confidence in the sovereignty of God sustained her during a time of great uncertainty.

This was something I tried to point out to Paula. My standard reply when she described yet another domestic tragedy was, "Remember, Paula, God is sovereign."

Paula's rejoinder would be, "Yes Larry, I know He's sovereign, but I don't want to hear about it at this time!" I learned quickly that a silent hug was better than a simplistic theological analysis.

Like many couples, Paula and I were opposites. Opposites not only attract, but also tend to rub on one another, especially in the Asian context. Adjusting to newly-wed life, a new baby and a scatterbrained husband didn't help matters either.

Most doors in Thailand use a latch instead of a door knob. On vacation I accidentally latched Paula in the bathroom on my way to lunch. As lunch started, I began to wonder why Paula was so late. A passerby happened to hear Paula beating on the door, "Help, help, I'm locked in the bathroom!" This good Samaritan went in, released the captive, and even said a special prayer for Paula's absent-minded husband!

One area where husband and wife must work to-gether is in child raising. Someone has said, "Isn't it humbling to see your own faults running around on two little legs?" When I was sick with typhoid at Manorom Hospital, Paula was in the thralls of morning sickness. Four- and two-year-old boys need a lot of scrutiny, but neither of us felt like playing nanny. Andy with his gen-erous heart and freedom to roam, decided to play Santa Claus and give toys to all the good little Thai boys and girls around the hospital. Andy's generosity was com-mendable, his thievery wasn't — the toys belonged to the guest house!

The hospital administrator was a most amiable fellow. His countenance definitely changed, however, when he found out about Andy's big "give-away". It was true; we had been irresponsible and lazy. We apologized to the administrator and promised to keep an eagle eye on the boys — especially "Santa".

During one particularly difficult time I received a letter from my eighty-year-old grandmother. Grandma was a charter member of a rural Baptist church founded in 1928. She had been a source of spiritual strength and encouragement to the family over the years. She wrote:

"I know God will give you strength and the courage to face the problems. There will be blessing too, I'm sure. I have lived in very primitive surroundings the first years of my marriage and that wasn't easy either. But I think it made me a stronger person even though I 'kicked against the pricks'. A soft, easy life doesn't do much for us; it only makes us more selfish and self-centered and sometimes snobbish."

Grandma closed the letter with this poem:

"For all the trials and tears of time,
For every hill I have to climb,
My heart sings but a grateful song;
These are the things that made me strong."

TWENTY ONE

FURLOUGH FEVER

A little girl was asked what she would like to be
if she could choose any occupation in the world.
She thought for a moment and then replied,
"a furloughing missionary."

Many people think of a furlough as an extended vacation. The little girl felt it was the next best thing to heaven. Webster furthers this idea by defining it as a "holiday or vacation". This is an unfortunate definition because a furlough is anything but a vacation and doesn't even come close to heaven. I have spoken to missionaries who have held over 300 meetings in one year. Some wives complain that they see more of their husbands on the field than they do on the homeside.

People tell me, "It must be nice to have such a nice break from your work."! On the contrary, near the end of furlough I actually began to look forward to returning to the field in order to get some rest. For this reason OMF has redefined furlough as *home assignment*, which stresses the fact that the work continues but in a different location.

In Singapore, the General Director warned us not to be missionaries who always kept a packed suitcase under the bed. We followed his advice and tried to make ourselves at home in the Thai context. But as home assignment drew near, our family contracted a strange disease — furlough fever. The symptoms were unmistakable: sweaty palms as we anticipated seeing relatives and friends; high pulse rates as we dreamed of Big Macs, rootbeers and tacos; and tightening in the chest as we contemplated leaving our Thai brethren for the uncertainties of re-entry into American society.

The long plane trip home was uneventful except for an encounter Andy had with an American soldier in Seoul, Korea. We were standing in line when Andy suddenly blurted out, "Look, Daddy, this man is a BLACK MAN!" I tried to explain to the soldier that Andy only knew Thai people and had never met a black person before. Obviously my children had a lot to learn about American culture.

After 24 hours in the air we arrived bleary-eyed and bone-tired at the Los Angeles International Airport. We must have been quite a sight; one disheveled missionary dragging eight bags of luggage, and a six-month-pregnant mother with two rowdy boys in tow. The customs official asked, "Residence?" Neither Paula nor I knew what to say. We had lost our identity. The official must have felt sorry for us; he sent us through without opening a single bag.

At the end of the ramp Paula's parents were waiting to take us to their palatial home in Orange County, California. The change from rice fields to the 42 miles of beaches along the Orange Riviera was dramatic. We went from our one-bedroom House of New Life into a four-bedroom mansion bordered by a canal with a 35-foot yacht. We were shocked to find that the neighbors actually left their lawn furniture out at night and it was still there the next morning!

That summer Paula found herself sunbathing at a country club, sipping Diet Coke and munching on a

Nestle's Crunch bar. She thought to herself, *Lord, this can't really be happening to me!* It took a while to get used to drinking tap water, driving on the "right" side of the road, cooking with microwaves, and eating rich food. We also had to adjust our sleeping habits. In Thailand we napped in the afternoon and turned in early at night. In America there were no more siestas, and at night it was so quiet we had trouble sleeping.

A further adjustment concerned TV. Four years in Asia effectively weaned us from the tube. It was just as well. The new programs left a lot to be desired. The first program I watched was, "The Lifestyles of the Rich and Famous". It showed the glamor and excesses of a billionaire sheik, movie star and divorce attorney. The program ended with Liberace who kept comparing the church to show business.

Disgusted with the program on lifestyles of the wealthy, I turned to Christian TV for relief, hoping for a contrasting and biblical viewpoint. The program was called, "Prosperity". The preacher spent half an hour convincing me that God wanted every Christian to be like Ben Franklin, "Healthy, wealthy, and wise." I wondered what the Lamnarai Christians would think of that theology. For them trusting Christ had brought persecution and ostracism, not success and prosperity. Four years in Thailand had obviously changed my perception of American life and culture. I was now seeing my home culture through the eyes of a Thai.

I also began to see the American church from a third world perspective. Driving along the interstate one day, I saw the gleaming roof of a church I had read about. Finding an exit, I slowly drove into the parking lot of the 22-acre complex. The church was covered with 10,500 two-by-six-foot glass cells, and had cost $16.5 million. Even Christians in Thailand had heard of this edifice and had asked us if we thought it was a good thing or not.

For the moment, the debate which surrounded the building was not important. All I could think of was the lean-to church I had left in Lamnarai. That church had no glass at all, much less stained glass, but it did have a nucleus of believers who loved the Lord and desired to see His Word spread. The truth of the saying, "A church is not a building, but people," was made real to me on that day.

After one month in California, we moved east to Shawnee, Oklahoma which would serve as our base for the next eleven months. The Lord provided a white frame house and two cars through relatives. A local cleaners even offered to do all our dry cleaning for free. Any fears we might have had concerning God's ability to provide were unfounded.

After I preached in one church a man came up to me and pressed a check for $500 into my hand. The parents of a sick child had vowed to the Lord that if their daughter lived, they would give any excess insurance money to the Lord's work. I happened to come to their church right after the little girl's recovery.

We were grateful that God was supplying so bountifully. In just four years prices had skyrocketed. Haircuts cost ten dollars, movies five dollars and a Big Mac $1.50. In Thailand I paid 75 cents for a haircut, shave, and massage, one dollar for a movie ticket and 50 cents for an entire meal. The first trip we took to a supermarket was a real revelation. Both sides of one forty-foot aisle were covered with breakfast cereals. In Thailand Paula made granola in our rather primitive oven but with mixed results. I wondered what our Thai dog Rolly would think of the dog food department. They even had one super premium dog food called Grand Gourmet which looked just like beef bourguignon. Mother Teresa observed, "The west is suffocating from muchness."

After some reflection I realized that America hadn't changed that much. I had changed. My attitudes and values were all affected by the missionary experience. Before leaving for the field, I had been a square peg in a square hole. Years in Thailand had worn off some of the edges and now the peg didn't fit so well. You might say I was a "misfit".

After a missions conference I stopped in at a pizza place for dinner. I was still wearing an Asian-style jacket from the conference. As I paid the bill and handed the cashier a tract, he gave me a strange look. Finally I explained myself and my dress.

"Oh I see," the cashier replied, "For a moment I thought you were part of the new age movement."

I thought to myself, *The **what** movement?"*

Actually, the Lord had prepared me for such shocks while still in Thailand. Once at the beach a Canadian teenage girl walked up and began to write "Beat it" in the sand.

I asked her, "What do you mean, 'Beat it'?"

She said, "Don't tell me you've never heard of Michael Jackson?" Michael Jackson had won eight Grammys and was world famous, but I remembered him merely as the fifth member of the Jackson Five.

Not all adjustments were negative. Paula adapted quickly to new products like liquid soap and pre-made pie dough. She enjoyed using a dishwasher and washer-dryer again. I enjoyed an office of my own, eating real meat loaf, driving a car, soaking in hot baths and preaching in "Okie" for a change. The children loved watching Sesame Street and Mr Rodgers, playing with transformers, building snowmen, and wearing socks. Andy fit quickly at kindergarten. At least there he was the same color and height as the other kids; he didn't have to wear a uniform and best of all, no one called him *farang,*

All missionaries look forward to church services in their native tongue. After giving out it is refreshing to be fed for a change. But when I read the bulletin our first Sunday back, I realized we were in the middle of a six-part series on 1 Corinthians 11. The subject? Veils. Issues on the field and back home were obviously poles apart.

The saturation of churches was also hard to get used to. Shawnee, a small county seat, had three times as many churches as Central Thailand and almost as many as Greater Bangkok. Among these churches there were hardly any with a real missions emphasis. When I told people where I worked some would say, "Is that so, where is *Thighland* anyway?" Most people's knowledge of Thailand was limited to Siamese cats, Siamese twins, and the musical *The King and I* (which is such a poor portrayal of the Thai monarchy that it is banned in Thailand). Educating and inspiring churches concerning missions was truly an uphill battle. At the same time we could always count on that rare individual or church to show genuine interest, experiences which made deputation well worthwhile.

Our twelve months homeside were full of highlights. None of them, however, could compare to the birth of Amber Elizabeth Dinkins in September of 1984, or Andy's second birth the following January. During the evening service one Sunday, five-year-old Andy was sitting in Paula's lap. Out of the blue he said, "I'd like to ask Jesus into my heart tomorrow."

Paula was surprised but told him, "You don't need to wait until tomorrow; you can trust Jesus tonight."

That winter the weather in Oklahoma was very cold. We had been telling Andy that those who truly trust

Jesus will go to heaven one day. He said, "Dad, I sure hope heaven is warmer than Oklahoma."

That same winter I was able to travel with J Oswald Sanders, past General Director of OMF and author of over 50 books. Mr Sanders was the main speaker at an OMF prayer conference I attended in Colorado. En route to Denver I lost my bags and had to wear the clothes on my back for a few days. Mr Sanders gave me one of his shirts and a pair of socks. I now understand Matthew 25:36, "naked and you clothed me." I told Paula of my intention to wear that shirt when I preached a sermon or wrote a book; hopefully some of Mr Sander's oratory and literary skill would rub off.

One disadvantage of traveling so much is finding time to minister in your own community. The Lord solved that problem by opening a door for ministry in the county jail. Mr Walter Walker had been visiting jails for 25 years and was happy to have me tag along. This is the poem he gave out to everyone he met:

> Lord, lay some soul upon my heart
> And love that soul through me,
> And help me nobly do my part,
> To win that soul to Thee.

The souls which the Lord especially laid on our hearts were Asians studying in my hometown. We were able to share the gospel for the first time with a girl from Mainland China and other students from Thailand and Laos. We also renewed friendship with the two Thai doctors in town, both of whom attended a Buddhist temple in Oklahoma City. It was interesting to hear that Buddhist temples had a kind of Sunday School where they taught songs like "Jesus Loves Me" but with a Buddhist twist: "Buddha loves me, this I know, for the Sutra tells me so ..."

I noticed quickly that such internationals were much more receptive to the gospel in their new environment. What's more, those that return to their home countries often become leaders in commerce, government and education. Internationals constitute a mission field right on the church's doorstep. Many churches seemed to be unaware of the opportunities to reach internationals, while others have learned to build bridges of friendship and as a result have led many to Christ.

1985 was the year of the Born Again Bunny (with John 3:3 tacked to its ear), Grace the Pro-life Doll and Christian aerobics called "The Firm Believer". The "name it claim it" craze was in full swing and the prosperity gospel was gaining its share of converts. Concerned about this, I wrote an article on simple lifestyle, which ended with this quote from the Lausanne Committee:

> All of us are shocked by the poverty of millions and disturbed by the injustices which cause it. Those of us who live in affluent circumstances accept our duty to develop a simple lifestyle in order to contribute more generously to both relief and evangelism.

Writing an article is one thing; living a simple life is quite another. This is particularly true when peers are climbing higher on the success ladder while we are staying on the lower rungs. A veteran missionary told me what to watch for on each furlough, "The first furlough your peers will have bought a house and a car. On the second furlough they will have moved into a larger house, the wife will be working and she'll have a car as well. On the third you'll notice that the carpets are thicker." As a missionary, I came to realize that God had not called me to a higher rung. I now know that contentment comes when I accept the rung God gives me. Paula found this concept hard to accept, especially after going through expensive wedding gifts we had stored in the attic for six years. She finally accepted the fact that some of them might never be used.

In the spring of 1985 furlough fever began to give way to Thai fever. We actually started looking forward to returning. Our sojourn in America was over: Thailand was our real home. Four-year-old Amber made this truth abundantly clear on a subsequent furlough when I noticed her crying for no apparent reason. "What's wrong, pumpkin?" I asked.

"I ... I miss my friends in Bangkop," was her tearful reply. It was true. Our children felt more at home in Asia; their schools were there and so were most of their friends. Not everyone shared our enthusiasm to return to Asia — especially relatives. Some dropped not-so-subtle hints that we should stay. When we shared with a relative the way God had used 1 Corinthians 1: 3-6 to comfort us during that difficult first term, he said, "I don't think it is God's will for you to go back. I think it is God's will for you to stay in Shawnee, and then you wouldn't need to be comforted or have your children suffer."

Despite such "helpful" advice, we knew deep inside it was time to depart. To stay home now would be like a medical student who finishes med school and residency and then refuses to practice medicine. Language school and internship was over; it was now time to practice wholeheartedly what we had learned.

In January of 1981, while we were still in Bangkok, the 52 American hostages held in Tehran, Iran, were released. Their homecoming, celebrated with tickertape parades and special ceremonies, was big news even in Thailand. A year later, in 1982, Vietnam veterans planned a massive reunion at the capital to celebrate a belated homecoming of their own. They did this to make up for the scorn and jeers they received from a disenchanted public during a very unpopular war.

A missionary from New Zealand experienced this contrast when flying home after a difficult term on the field. On his plane was the famous New Zealand All Blacks rugby team, returning from a victorious tour. At the airport they were met by an enthusiastic crowd who admired the trophy they had won. As the dejected missionary walked down the ramp, he commented to his wife, "Some homecoming this is, there isn't one soul here to welcome us."

His wife, noticing the dejection in his voice, said, "Yes, darling, but remember we're not *home* yet."

During our twelve months stateside I had to remind myself that I wasn't home yet. I may never get the reception of a victorious football team or liberated hostage on this earth, but one day there will be a glorious Homecoming. The difference is that that Homecoming will have no end.

CONCLUSION

In 1979 Tom Wolfe published a bestseller on the NASA space program called The Right Stuff. Wolfe's goal was to capture the character of that elite group of pilots who through sheer determination and tireless devotion became America's first astronauts. Pilots who possessed such prerequisites were said to have the right stuff.

"As to just what this ineffable quality was . . . well, it obviously involved bravery. But it was not bravery in the simple sense of being willing to risk your life . . . No, the idea here seemed to be that a man should have the ability to go up in a hurtling piece of machinery and put his hide on the line . . . and then go up again the next day, and the next day . . . and ultimately, in its best expression, do so in a cause that means something to thousands, to a people, a nation, to humanity, to God."

(Tom Wolfe)[1]

Missionary biographies and textbooks on missions often give the impression that the right stuff for foreign service includes extraordinary gifts or talents and borders on sainthood. A term in Thailand taught me otherwise. It is not necessary to be a linguist, anthropologist, theologian or even evangelist to qualify as a missionary. A willingness to laugh at yourself and flow with sometimes

---

[1] *The Right Stuff, Farror Straus Giroux, New York 1979, pg 24*

unpleasant surroundings is more important than de-grees, special skills or natural talents. As with all of us, God is not so concerned with our ability as He is our availability.

In our case, God took two inexperienced yet willing missionaries through a series of ups and downs, victories and defeats. Like ingredients in a cake, these experi-ences, both the bitter and the sweet, blended together to make an eventful first term. Somehow, in the midst of all our fumbling and bumbling, the church in Lamnarai was planted.

Ezekiel 17:10 asks, "Behold, though it is planted will it thrive?" We asked the same question when we left Lamnarai in 1984. The church was planted but would it prosper? Would it continue to grow or wither under opposition? After six years the Lamnarai Church has not only survived, it has flourished.

Lamnarai, however, is only one of 685 district towns in Thailand, the majority of which lack a resident gospel witness. Over half of the 65 district towns in Central Thailand are still waiting for a church to be planted there. My prayer is that this book will not only move people to intercede for this needy portion of God's field, but to join in the work towards what many feel will be a great harvest.

One such visionary was Puan Akkapin, past director of the Church of Christ in Thailand (Presbyterian). He said, "I believe one hundred percent that Thailand will become Christian . . . It is possible that thousands of my people will become Christians in a wave of conversions which will shake this nation. It is my faith absolutely that this day is coming."

The wave of conversions Puang longed for has yet to occur, but we do see the ripples of revival lapping on the Thai shore. Reports from various parts of the country indicate that the winds of renewal are blowing. Such individual conversions are encouraging, but what we long for is a people movement with whole families, villages, and communities turning to Christ.

To help sharpen our vision, the Thai delegation to Lausanne II established the following goals for Thailand by the year 2000: 600,000 Christians, 6,000 churches, and 6,000 pastors. This means the Thai church will need to increase *sixfold* over the next decade! Such an increase demands a corresponding rise in the number of church planters, Bible schools, and institutions in which to train and equip the influx of new believers. How can Thai Christians the less than one percent of the population hope to achieve such lofty goals? The answer is found in Christ's command of Matthew 9:38: ". . . beg the Lord of the harvest to send out workers into His harvest."

This book demonstrates that those who answer the call to work in God's harvest fields will need to make many adjustments, especially in the first few years. This truth was confirmed again to me through a painfully honest letter written by a new worker in Central Thailand. We had corresponded with Martin (mentioned in the introduction) and Barbara Stidham and had followed with interest their progress through Singapore, Study House and eventually designation to the district town of Angthong to work with the Curtises. Barbara wrote describing their first month up country:

"When we moved into our Thai wooden slat house there were holes in the floor and no screens. This meant that we were visited often by mice, cockroaches, toads, flies and mosquitos. My biggest adjustment has been to the 100 degree heat, especially in our 'sauna' — kitchen area covered by galvanized roofing. My supervisor described our house as 'humble'. I just wish my heart was as humble as this house! We were scheduled to study language six hours a day but for the first four days our language helpers did not show up. Then, after five days, our housegirl quit. On top of that Martin has dengue fever with 104° and I am nauseated daily, sometimes all day with morning sickness."

After reading Barbara's letter I wrote back, "Angthong is supposed to mean 'Golden Bowl', but for you it seems to have turned into an 'Affliction Bowl'. Your description of your 'humble' home brings back (not-so-fond) memories. Problems with the heat, critters, housegirls and language helpers are all too familiar. I can especially identify with Martin's dengue and Paula with Barbara's nausea. Your description of your 'sauna' fits our kitchen in Lamnarai to a T. I'm glad you see this experience as a character building time. Get ready, this may be the first such trying experience as a church planter, but it won't be your last."

What impressed me most about Barbara's letter was not the similarities to our first term, but the spiritual lessons they were learning through various trials. Barbara ended her letter by quoting 1 Corinthians 15:58 and reflecting: "I hope we're becoming more like Jesus and developing attitudes of gratitude rather than complaining. We are not there yet!"

Our family would agree with the Stidhams. We are not there yet either. A decade of missionary service has yet to produce a single feather or even the hint of a halo. What it has produced is a greater desire to be, as Barbara put it, "more like Jesus." When all is said and done, that is all that really matters anyway. Whether we labor on a foreign shore or "stand by the stuff" at home, our ultimate goal should be the same: conformity to the image and likeness of Christ.

Reliving the events of our first term has been both an

emotional and spiritual exercise. My flesh resisted dig-
ging up the bones of robbery and sickness from a
painful past, but those experiences were more than
balanced by the glimmers of spiritual interest and the
joy of conversions. Such victories were inevitably followed by defeats, yet failure gave us a fresh opportunity
to trust in God's wisdom, not our own. Furthermore,
each new beginning proved to be a stepping stone to a
deeper relationship with the Saviour. We learned that
change is not always bad. Through it we have come to a
better understanding of ourselves, a broader knowledge
of God's Word and most of all a deeper appreciation of
God's love for sinful man.

FOR FURTHER THOUGHT AND ACTION...

Chapter 1

Courtship (page 1)

1. *Why is a Biblical foundation important, no matter what occupation you choose? (p.3)*

2. *List reasons why you would not like to be a missionary. (p.3)*

3. *Why is it important to have up-to-date information on those you intercede for? (p.3)*

Chapter 2

Engagement (page 8)

1. *Is the "call to missions" different from the call to a secular occupation or to some other home side ministry? (p.9)*

2. *Are you involved in a missionary prayer group of "like minded friends"? What can you do in your church or community to encourage such a meeting? (p.12)*

3. *Why is it necessary for a wife to be accepted on her own merits? (p.13)*

Chapter 3

Honeymoon Begins (page 16)

1. *What is meant by "Be a missionary who oils the works, not grit"? (p.18)*

184

Chapter 4

The Honeymoon Ends (page 22)

Chapter 5

A Ponderous Body (page 29)

Chapter 6

Protestant Cemetery (page 37)

2. *Read Hebrews 11 and John 12:24 in light of this chapter.*

3. *What lessons did God teach you through this cemetery classroom? (p.44)*

Chapter 7

Mecca of Buddhism (page 45)

1 *Review the problems of using John 3:16 in a Buddhist context. (p.46)*

2. *How would you respond to the Lunatic, Liar and Lord illustration? (p.47)*

3. *Why is it important to check out "professions of faith" in Thailand? (p.50)*

Chapter 8

Greenhorns and Tenderfoots (page 53)

1. *How would you explain to someone how disciples are developed? (p.53)*

2. *Have you ever said "I'll never do that", only to find yourself in the exact situation? What was God trying to teach you? (p.57)*

3. *Review the courtship - engagement - honeymoon illustration shown in chapters 1-8. How does it fit in with your situation? Where are you in the process?*

Chapter 9

Dark Places of the Earth (page 59)

1. *Read Thomas Ragland's quote again: how do you*

gauge the "opportunities for usefulness" at home and overseas? (p.59)

2. *Why was Central Thailand called a missionary graveyard? (p.60)*

3. *What qualities are necessary in "trail blazing" or pioneer situations? (p.61)*

Chapter 10

Church Planting 101 (page 66)

1. *Review the six statements made by David Pickard. Why do you think these are important to mission work? (p.68)*

2. *Can a missionary really expect to plant a church in his first term? Why do you think it would be possible and why do you think it would be hard? (p.66)*

3. *Why was the "amphur" strategy implemented in Central Thailand? How does this fit in with Paul's method of church planting? (p.69)*

Chapter 11

Droppings of the Angels (page 74)

1. *Look up "leprosy" in an encyclopaedia or Bible dictionary. What are some characteristics of this disease? (p.74)*

2. *What lesson on contentment does Mr Hit's testimony teach us? (p.80)*

3. *What is the difference between "healing" and "cleansing"? (p.82)*

Chapter 12

The First Six Months (page 83)

1. *What does Satan hope to attain by attacking especially the newer missionaries?*

2. *Re-read the verses quoted on p.89 and evaluate your own attitude towards material possessions.*

3. *How should we pray for missionaries during those critical first six months? (p.93)*

Chapter 13

Culture Shock (page 94)

1. *Re-read the poem on p.94. What was Kipling trying to communicate in that stanza?*

2. *Why does "It is not wrong it is just different" really mean? (p.102)*

3. *What is your definition of culture shock? (p.103)*

Chapter 14

No Big Names (page 104)

1. *Why does God delight in using the foolish and weak to confound the wise and strong? (p.104)*

2. *Why is it important that a new missionary take the role of learner rather than teacher?*

Chapter 15

Lamnarai Lab (page 109)

1. *How should missionaries respond to "well meaning" supporters who criticize them? (p.115)*

2. *Why do praying and fasting work when other methods fail? (p.118)*

3. *Someone has said discouragement is the missionary's greatest enemy. Why is this often true? (p.115-116)*

Chapter 16

God's Megaphone (page 119)

1. Has C. S. Lewis' quote been true in your experience? (p.119)

2. Think of a recent affliction you have endured. How did you benefit from that experience?

3. What is the meaning of "rice or quinine Christians"? Do we have similar type Christians in our home countries? (p.120)

Chapter 17

House of New Life (page 128)

1. *What did you learn about "identification" from this chapter? (p.128)*

2. *Are imitating and identifying the same? If not how are they different?*

3. *Is Ada Lum's quote on p.136 just for missionaries or for every Christian?*

Chapter 18

MKS - Missionary Kids (page 138)

1. *Why is MK education the most difficult problem for married missionaries?*

2. *What does a "National Geographic" Christian mean? (p.138)*

3. *What does Mark 10:29-30 mean when it says that those who have "left" will receive a hundred times as much.....?*

Chapter 19

Good sense of humour, bad sense of smell (page 148)

1. *List reasons why a sense of humour is necessary on the field?*

2. *Would your friend characterise you as the serious or "laid back" type? What areas do you tend to be too serious about? What can you do in order to "lighten up"?*

3. *What stories in the scriptures amuse you? Discuss with some friends some of those stories.*

Chapter 20

Do Missionaries Have Halos? (page 157)

1. *Why should we not put missionaries on a pedestal? (p.157)*

2. *Why was Isobel Kuhn surprised by the discovery of "scum" in her life? (p.158)*

3. *Why is an identity crisis often more traumatic than culture shock? (p.160)*

Chapter 21

Furlough Fever (page 168)

1. *Look up "furlough" in a dictionary. Why is that definition less than suitable for the average missionary on home leave?*

2. *What can a church do for missionaries on home assignment? What do you think they need the most?*

3. *How can we determine biblically what our level of lifestyle should be? Reflect on the Lausanne Committee statement on p.175. What exactly is a "simple lifestyle"?*